THE GREAT COOKS' GUIDE TO

# Appetizers

# GREAT COOKS' LIBRARY

America's leading food authorities share their home-tested recipes and expertise on cooking equipment and techniques

THE GREAT COOKS' GUIDE TO

# Appetizers

A BEARD GLASER WOLF BOOK

RANDOM HOUSE, NEW YORK

**Front Cover** (left to right, top to bottom): Spanakopita, page 32; Curry Turnovers, page 33; Yogurt Cheese with Scallions and Walnuts, page 21; Assorted Canapes, page 13.

**Back Cover** (left to right, top to bottom): Ham Mousse, page 23; Fried Fontina, page 42 *(deep fryer courtesy Charles F. Lamalle);* Cheese-Stuffed Triangles and Snails, page 30; Shrimp Scandia, page 46; *(aspic/canape cutters courtesy La Cuisiniere).*

**Interior Photographs:** Page 4, *hotray courtesy Salton, Inc.;* Page 5 (top), *chafing dish courtesy Hammacher Schlemmer;* Page 7, *food processor courtesy Farberware;* Page 8 (top), *deep fryer courtesy Charles F. Lamalle, thermometer courtesy Taylor Instruments.*

Book Design by Milton Glaser, Inc.

Cover Photograph by Richard Jeffery

Food Styling by Lucy Wing
Props selected by Yvonne McHarg and Beard Glaser Wolf Ltd.

Library of Congress Cataloguing in Publication Data

Main entry under title:

The Great Cooks' Guide to Appetizers.
(The Great Cooks' Library)
1. Cookery (Appetizers)    I. Series.
TX740.G68      641.8'12      77-90242
ISBN: 0-394-73607-9

Manufactured in the United States of America
2 4 6 8 9 7 5 3
First Edition

We have gathered together some of the great cooks in this country to share their recipes—and their expertise—with you. As you read the recipes, you will find that in certain cases techniques will vary. This is as it should be: Cooking is a highly individual art, and our experts have arrived at their own personal methods through years of experience in the kitchen.

THE EDITORS

## SENIOR EDITORS

Wendy Afton Rieder
Kate Slate

## ASSOCIATE EDITORS

Lois Bloom
Susan Lipke

## EDITORIAL ASSISTANT

Christopher Carter

## PRODUCTION MANAGER

Emily Aronson

## EDITORIAL STAFF

Mardee Haidin
Michael Sears
Patricia Thomas

## CONTRIBUTORS

## Introduction by Lyn Stallworth

**Eliza and Joshua Baer** have worked in various phases of the restaurant business on the West Coast and are currently planning a cookbook.

**Michael Batterberry,** author of several books on food, art and social history, is also a painter, and is editor and food critic for a number of national magazines. He has taught at James Beard's cooking classes in New York and many of his original recipes have appeared in *House & Garden, House Beautiful* and *Harper's Bazaar.*

**Paula J. Buchholz** is the regional co-ordinator for the National Culinary Apprenticeship Program. She has been a food writer for the *Detroit Free Press* and for the *San Francisco Examiner.*

**Vilma Liacouras Chantiles,** author of *The Food of Greece,* writes a food and consumer column for the *Scarsdale* (New York) *Inquirer* and a monthly food column for the *Athenian Magazine* (Athens, Greece).

**Ruth Ellen Church,** a syndicated wine columnist for the *Chicago Tribune,* had been food editor for that newspaper for more than thirty years when she recently retired. The author of seven cookbooks, her most recent books are *Entertaining with Wine* and *Wines and Cheese of the Midwest.*

**Elizabeth Schneider Colchie** is a noted food consultant who has done extensive recipe development and testing as well as research into the history of foods and cookery. She was on the editorial staff of *The Cooks' Catalogue* and *The International Cooks' Catalogue* and has written numerous articles for such magazines as *Gourmet, House & Garden* and *Family Circle.*

**Isabel S. Cornell**, a home economist, was Associate Editor for the revised edition of *Woman's Day Encyclopedia of Cookery* and Special Projects Editor for the revised edition of *Woman's Day Collector's Cook Book.* While on the *Woman's Day* staff, she selected, tested and judged for their recipe contests.

**Carol Cutler**, who has been a food columnist for the *Washington Post*, is a graduate of the Cordon Bleu and L'Ecole des Trois Gourmands in Paris. She is the author of *Haute Cuisine for Your Heart's Delight* and *The Six-Minute Soufflé and Other Culinary Delights.* She has also written for *House & Garden, American Home* and *Harper's Bazaar.*

**Florence Fabricant** is a free-lance writer, reporting on restaurants and food for *The New York Times, New York* magazine and other publications. She was on the staff of *The Cooks' Catalogue* and editor of the paperback edition. She also contributed to *The International Cooks' Catalogue* and *Where to Eat in America.*

**Emanuel and Madeline Greenberg** co-authored *Whiskey in the Kitchen* and are consultants to the food and beverage industry. Emanuel, a home economist, is a regular contributor to the food columns of *Playboy* magazine. Both contribute to *House Beautiful, Harper's Bazaar* and *Travel & Leisure.*

**Mireille Johnston**, the author of *The Cuisine of the Sun*, a cookbook of Provençal specialties, is currently completing a book on the cooking of Burgundy, *The Cuisine of the Rose.*

**Matt Kramer** writes a food column for the *Willamette Week* in Portland, Oregon.

**Jeanne Lesem**, Family Editor of United Press International, is the author of *The Pleasures of Preserving and Pickling.*

**Florence Lin** has been teaching Chinese cooking at the China Institute in New York for 17 years. She is the author of *Florence Lin's Chinese Regional Cookbook* and *Florence Lin's Chinese Vegetarian Cookbook* and was the chief food consultant for the *Cooking of China* in Time-Life Books' *Foods of the World* series.

**Susan Lipke** is an Associate Editor of the Great Cooks' Library series as well as *The International Cooks' Catalogue* and *The Cooks' Catalogue.*

**Nan Mabon**, a free-lance food writer and cooking teacher in New York City, is also the cook for a private executive dining room on Wall Street. She studied at the Cordon Bleu in London.

**Mitsuo Masuzawa** has been a chef at the Kitcho Restaurant in New York City since 1970.

**Gloria Bley Miller** is the author of *Learn Chinese Cooking in Your Own Kitchen* and *The Thousand Recipe Chinese Cookbook*.

**Maurice Moore-Betty**, owner-operator of The Civilized Art Cooking School, food consultant and restaurateur, is author of *Cooking for Occasions, The Maurice Moore-Betty Cooking School Book of Fine Cooking* and *The Civilized Art of Salad Making*.

**Jane Moulton**, a food writer for the *Plain Dealer* in Cleveland, took her degree in foods and nutrition. As well as reporting on culinary matters and reviewing food-related books for the *Plain Dealer*, she has worked in recipe development, public relations and catering.

**Robert Renaud**, owner and chef of Le Jacques Coeur in New York City, began his apprenticeship at l'Escargot in Bourges, France, in 1936, and has worked in many restaurants since then in the French provinces and in Paris, England and the United States.

**Paul Rubinstein** is the author of *Feasts for Two, The Night Before Cookbook* and *Feasts for Twelve (or More)*. He is a stockbroker and the son of pianist Artur Rubinstein.

**Maria Luisa Scott and Jack Denton Scott** co-authored the popular *Complete Book of Pasta* and have also written many other books on food, including *Informal Dinners for Easy Entertaining, Mastering Microwave Cooking, The Best of the Pacific Cookbook,* and *Cook Like a Peasant, Eat Like a King*. With the renowned chef Antoine Gilly, they wrote *Feast of France*.

**Satish Sehgal** is the founder of the successful Indian Oven restaurant in New York City, which specializes in northern Indian cuisine. He began developing recipes for northern specialties while an engineering student in southern India and later abandoned engineering for the food world.

**Ruth Spear** is the author of *The East Hampton Cookbook* and writes occasional pieces on food for *New York* magazine. She is currently at work on a new cookbook.

**Marion Lear Swaybill**, a field producer-writer in the documentary division of NBC News in New York, long ago took up cooking as a serious avocation and has become an expert cook and baker.

**Paula Wolfert**, author of *Mediterranean Cooking* and *Couscous and Other Good Food from Morocco*, is also a cooking teacher and consultant. She has written articles for *Vogue* and other magazines.

**Nicola Zanghi** is the owner-chef of Restaurant Zanghi in Glen Cove, New York. He started his apprenticeship under his father at the age of thirteen, and is a graduate of two culinary colleges. He has been an instructor at the Cordon Bleu school in New York City.

# Contents

# FRITTERS AND OTHER FRIED HORS D'OEUVRES

# VEGETABLE, EGG AND SEAFOOD APPETIZERS

# HOT MEAT APPETIZERS

# Appetizers

What Americans mean when they say "appetizer" is a finger food, or at least a bit of food easily handled, served at gatherings and parties. Until this century, the drink-and-tidbit ritual was a men-only affair—the women may have prepared the dozens of little dishes that make up the *mezzes* that Greek and Turkish men downed with their *ouzo* or *raki* as they watched the sun set into the Aegean, but they didn't join the men to savor those olives, bits of fried fish, or sizzling cheese. The same held true in Spain where the copious array of snacks called *tapas*—the name is derived from slices of bread placed over sherry glasses to protect the contents from flies—are spread out in bars, where only recently no self-respecting *senõra* would show her face. And of course turn-of-the-century ladies—*if* they were ladies—never got a crack at the fabulous free lunch laid out in the best saloons.

Now that women have won the freedom to enter bars, what they'll usually find as accompaniment to drinks are bowls of dry-roasted nuts or little pretzels. Nothing is wrong with that, but anyone in search of appetizers as they should and can be, piping hot or crisply chilled, will usually find them only in private homes.

Many people use the French term, *hors d'oeuvre*, when referring to an appetizer. Strictly speaking, an *hors d'oeuvre*—which means "outside the work," the "work" being the main meal—is a first course, served at table. A better French equivalent of appetizer would be *amuse-gueule*, "mouth-amuser," or *bonne-bouche*, a pleasing mouthful. Sophisticated French will often use the Russian word *zakouska*, which signifies a dollop of caviar or a morsel of smoked salmon, perhaps placed on a small slice of black bread and accompanied by ice-cold vodka. By now *zakouska* and its plural *zakouski* are part of the vocabulary of fashionable Paris, used when finger-food is served.

Some form of appetizer really is necessary when drinks are served, to keep the conversational ball rolling and the guests upright. Those who don't drink alcohol appreciate a bit of food as much as the topers! The food needn't be elaborate—an assortment of nuts and olives, whole wheat, sesame or rye crackers, a dip, a wedge of cheese—any or all of these would please a few friends having a drink together. If dinner will be delayed for some reason, extra ballast can be added to an appetizer assortment. It's a matter of judgment, deciding what will keep guests feeling happy without losing their anticipation of dinner; they should not be suffering dire hunger pangs when they reach the table, but neither should they arrive so stuffed that food no longer has appeal. How many of us have spent days in loving but arduous preparation of our special dishes, then found we've let our guests fill up on so many pre-dinner tidbits that their appetites are sated? It's better to be austere rather than lavish before a meal—your guests will be grateful when they see the main course.

There is, however, an occasion when appetizers can very well be the meal, as guests choose or not, and that is the great American institution, the cocktail party. This form of entertaining allows you to play host to a maximum number of guests without an enormous expenditure of money or effort. Cocktail parties are free-wheeling affairs where guests can drop in on their way to other parties or dinners, or stay to make an evening of it. There should be a variety of food to suit both sets—pickled mushrooms or shrimp for the couple who have done two parties and have another one ahead of them, and lots of rib-stickers for the old pals who have dug in for the duration.

For a large party of 25 to 100 guests, almost any food that can be eaten without fuss qualifies as an appetizer. Often it's the size of the serving that distinguishes appetizer from main course, such as tiny, bite-sized quiches instead of the luncheon pie-wedge, or half-dollar sized rounds of beef, ham or chicken on miniature bread slices instead of man-sized sandwiches.

Without a lot of elaborate preparation, a selection of appetizers can be drawn from around the world. For example, take a category as basic as the dip. To transport guests to the south of France, serve aïoli, a garlic-laden mayonnaise, with strips of fresh raw vegetables. Or move on to the Middle East, with the chick-pea and sesame paste spread called *hummus bi tahini*, scooped up with toasted bits of *pita* bread. If the mood is Mexican, have *guacamole* with tortilla chips. For finger food, try Indian *samosas*, Chinese tea eggs, or Dutch meat balls. Even if there is no time to prepare appetizers, an international delicatessen can be set out with such foods as salami from Genoa, vine leaves from Greece, cheese from Denmark and crackers from England. And remember that the great Escoffier recommended serving sardines in their can!

Whether appetizers are plain or fancy, international or down-home, a few planning guidelines are imperative. First, eliminate any foods that might appear at dinner. If cheese soufflé with a tomato sauce is on the menu, neither cheese nor tomatoes should be served in any form with drinks. In cold weather, especially, its nice to have at least one hot appetizer, such as small squares of spinach pie or curry turnovers. Keep in mind the contrast of flavors and textures. A rough pâté should be presented along with a smooth dip like carp-roe *taramosalata*. Spicy and mild foods might be offered to the same group—those who find cheese straws with cayenne a bit too peppery would be pleased to opt for some cheese mousse or cheese puffs. Bear in mind that sweet and sour foods—barbecued ribs and pickled vegetables—complement one another.

Elizabeth David, whom many consider the finest food writer in the English language, feels that the ideal assortment of foods before a meal would have "something raw, something salty, something dry or meaty, something gentle and smooth and possibly something in the way of fresh

2

fish." According to taste, the meal to follow, the season of the year, and what's available, her suggestion could be followed by serving cherry tomatoes with an anchovy mayonnaise, slices of cold cuts, a ham mousse and shrimps Scandia. The results would be simple, balanced and delicious —and not too much.

**Planning.** How appetizers are chosen depends a lot upon the occasion. When you begin to plan, ask yourself: Will you call a definite halt to the party, or keep open house all evening? How large is the party? When those questions are answered, the decks are cleared for easy planning.

If the party precedes a meal, count on—roughly—five light appetizers per person. Remember that the count of five per person is only an approximation, though usually the hearty eaters compensate for the picky ones. If you are preparing for a long night, be sure to have a few substantial appetizers such as cheese and spinach pie, individual pizzas, or rough country pâté. In this case, you can reckon on an average of eight to ten appetizers per head, including both heavy and light offerings. How much variety is offered will depend on your time and the number of guests expected—the more people, the likelier you'll be to prepare a number of items. However, two appetizers of good quality are far preferable to four or five dishes needing last minute attention that will leave you harried and in the kitchen.

Do as much as possible ahead of time. Prepared pastries can be ready to pop into the oven, some canapés and sandwiches, if not too moist, can sit overnight in the refrigerator covered with plastic wrap or a damp tea towel, as can pâtés and dips. Canapés, pâtés and some dips should be brought to near room temperature before serving.

**Serving Appetizers.** If planning a party for 20 or more with several hot dishes among the appetizers, it pays to seriously consider having someone to heat and pass food and tidy up in general. Whether or not help is on hand, some thought should be given to the presentation of appetizers. A plate of good food is quickly devastated, and if left in view looks mighty forlorn. It's best to arrange an appetizer on several plates, keeping some in the kitchen as replacements for those that are emptied. That is easier than rummaging in the kitchen to replenish a single dish, and the switch keeps the living room tidy and you with your guests.

Artistic people can arrange a food tray almost by instinct, and need no help. The rest of us can use suggestions. In general, if the garnishes are themselves edible—like parsley sprigs, bunches of watercress and carrot curls—they provide necessary accents along with a perky, palatable appearance. A fine sprinkling of chopped parsley, dill or paprika can work wonders to relieve pallid stuffed eggs, or what appears to be the snowfield of a yogurt dip, as well as give a lift to mayonnaise-based dips. A wonderful bit of kitchen frippery that will make garnishing with chopped fresh herbs a great deal easier is a hand-cranked parsley mincer, but nothing excells a food processor for this task, if you're lucky enough to have one. And, if your tastes—and pocketbook—run to the crème de la crème of garnishes, a set of truffle cutters will produce many small and ele-

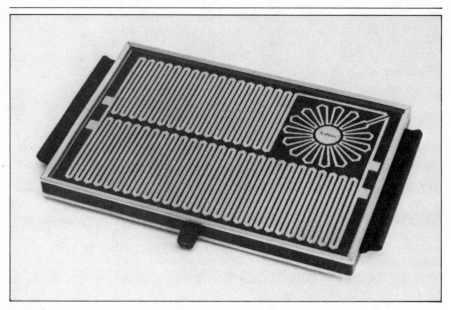

**Hot tray.** A practical way to keep several hors d'oeuvres warm is provided by a large electric food warmer. The heat is adjustable, and one corner is reserved for dishes that need to be extra-hot, such as a mulled cider or a melted cheese dip. The glass surface cleans easily.

gant shapes out of that expensive fungus or out of egg whites, olives, carrots or other firm foods.

To protect precious silver trays, line them with a deep bed of lettuce or bread before arranging any acidic food on them. Electric hot trays or chafing dishes will keep hot appetizers warm, and set out plenty of small napkins. Ashtrays liberally disposed about the room will give guests a place to stow the inevitable appetizer toothpicks and obviate the shock of finding a forest of them, the morning after, in the philodendron. To encourage guests to circulate, place food at a number of different strategic points. When it's appropriate, have salt shakers and pepper mills handy.

**Types of Appetizers.** Size is the common denominator of an appetizer. One, or at most two, mouthfuls is the limit. And the morsel should be, insofar as possible, non-drippy.

**Canapes.** *Canape* in French means sofa, and presumably these tiny open-faced sandwiches were so dubbed because the topping that sits on its bed of toast reminded an anonymous wit of a person perched on a piece of furniture. The base can be melba toast, a cracker or biscuit, small "party-sized" rye, or the traditional white or brown bread spread with butter and

**Copper chafing dish.** Chafing dishes look great and keep hot appetizers nice and warm. This one, made of copper for good heat transmission, has a basin of hot water between food and fire to prevent scorching, a strong frame for stability and an adjustable alcohol burner.

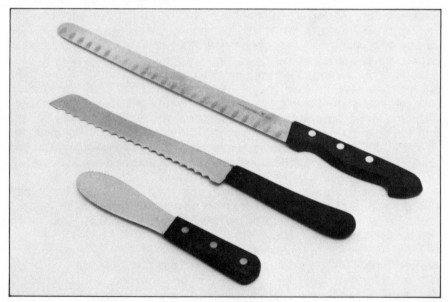

**Ham slicer, bread knife and sandwich spreader.** Hollow-ground ovals on one long blade make it efficient for slicing roast meats; deep serrations on another long blade aid in slicing bread; and a short, broad-bladed knife with one serrated edge will smooth spreads and trim garnishes.

toasted on one side. If possible, buy unsliced loaves (or bake crustless pullman loaves) and, with a good serrated bread knife, cut them, lengthwise and horizontally, into ¼''-thick slices. Then use a knife or variously shaped canapé cutters to achieve various shapes. Set up a small assembly line: Toast the bread, if desired, or make oven-crisped croutons by placing the cut-outs on buttered baking sheets and toasting them in a preheated 450 F. oven for about eight minutes. To decorate canapés, use a sandwich spreader, or a pastry bag where it's appropriate, and have all toppings at room temperature. Bread-based canapés can be frozen for several weeks, but without mayonnaise, which will separate and turn dark. Take them out of the freezer about two hours before serving time, and heat them in the oven or broiler, preferably in relays as needed.

Possible toppings for canapés stretch as far as the imagination. Avoid spreading moist toppings until the last possible minute, and garnish the canapés as they are arranged on serving plates.

For hot canapés, don't forget that frozen muffin, biscuit, puff pastry, or croissant dough from the market can give excellent results in jig time.

**Canapé Offshoots.** "Jelly roll" sandwiches, the layers sliced lengthwise from very fresh unsliced loaves, rolled around a filling then sliced in rounds, are a lot of trouble and worth every bit of it. As the ads say, it shows guests that you care. If a lid is put on a canapé, it is technically a tea sandwich, but why quibble? Try tiny *croque monsieurs*, thin slices of ham and Gruyère between rounds of fine-textured, trimmed white bread, spread on the outside with a little butter and baked until the cheese melts.

**Dips.** The ubiquitous sour cream and dried onion soup number that we all know well stayed on the top of the charts for so long because it was a cinch to prepare and really not bad at all. Sour cream remains a wonderful dip base—and so does yogurt—but with a food processor, mayonnaise, cottage cheese and butter bases can be turned out, flavored as desired, with a flick of the switch. The processor works with the speed of light, but for garlic-flavored *aïoli* and *hummus bi tahini*, traditionalists insist that a mortar and pestle releases the garlic oils gently as no mechanical means can. However, if the garlic can "rest" in the dip for several hours, the food processor's results are quite satisfactory.

Be sure that any pieces of bread, cracker or tortilla that accompany a dip are firm enough not to break off and float soggily on the surface. If crackers have lost their bounce, crisp them in a 250 F. oven for ten minutes or so.

**Vegetables.** There's no need to confine vegetable appetizers to celery, carrots, cherry tomatoes, cucumber and green pepper strips, refreshing and healthful as they are. Try flowerets of cauliflower or very fresh broccoli, the tenderest part of tiny artichoke leaves, or chunks of jicama (if you have access to that popular West Coast mild and crunchy root). Strips of fennel, asparagus tips and Belgian endive leaves are also incredibly good with hot or cold, mild or spicy dips. Use a hollowed-out red or green cab-

**Food processor.** Hours of chopping, slicing, shredding, mincing and grating can be saved by an electric food processor with interchangeable cutting disks and blades. This versatile machine is also ideal for making herb butters, dips, pâtés and smooth cheese spreads for canapés.

bage framed by some of its outspread leaves to hold a dip; it makes a fine centerpiece at the same time. Some cooks prefer to blanch vegetables in lots of boiling water for a few minutes, refresh them in cold water, then chill them before serving. The partially-cooked vegetables are brightly colored, and can be pickled à *la grêque*, or served in the same way as raw *crudités*. Needless to say, vegetable appetizers appeal to the diet-conscious.

Store the vegetables unwashed in the refrigerator, and wash them as close to preparation as possible lest they wilt. Soak broccoli, cauliflower and cabbage in salted, acidulated water for at least a half hour to coax out any insect life they might harbor. Use a sharp paring knife or special tool to cut radishes into roses. If you like, soak the vegetables in iced water for at least an hour before serving, and if you have a rimmed container and a friend or helper with a watchful eye who will drain it when necessary, serve the vegetables on a bed of crushed ice.

**Deep Frying.** People who shy away from ordering fried foods in restaurants are only too happy to encounter deep-fried clam fritters at a cocktail gathering; after all, *one* fritter can't really do too much damage to the figure! (The fact that few of us can stop at one is beside the point.)

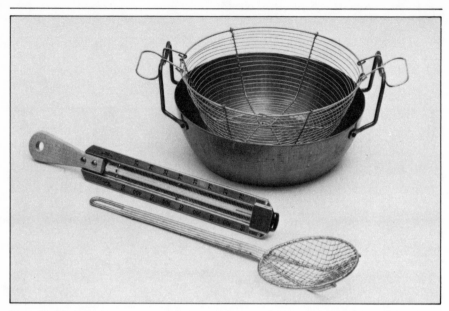

**Deep fryer, thermometer and skimmer.** For success in deep frying, use a broad, heavy pot that holds and distributes heat well, like this steel one, an accurate thermometer that clips on the pot and registers to at least 400 F. and a long wire skimmer or basket to lift and drain the fried food.

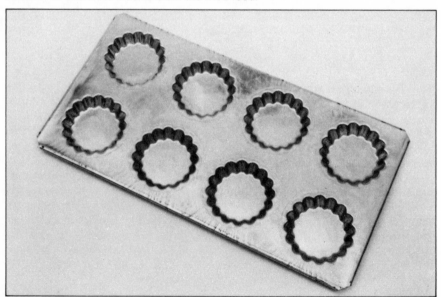

**Tinned-steel tartlet pan.** Savory tarts with scalloped edges can be quickly made in a molded pan, which is easier to handle than individual tins sliding around on a baking sheet. Rolled-out dough, cut into circles, is pressed into the shallow indentations to form 8 shells.

**The Right Oil.** The best choice is a bland vegetable oil such as corn or peanut oil, which heats to the proper frying temperature of 350 to 400 F. without smoking or smelling. Lard is out of favor as frying media for reasons of arterial health, and olive oil is too strongly flavored for many palates and dishes.

Purists say that oil should be strained directly after use to remove any particles that might burn when it is reheated, and that the oil should be used only twice because it can quickly become rancid. Be sure to skim off any large particles floating in the oil at any time to prevent burning and changing the flavor of the oil. It should be stored in a cool place. Needless to say, use the oil in which fish is fried only for fish.

There are a number of fine deep fryers with basket inserts on the market. A deep-fryer should be heavy and large enough so that when it is only half full it will contain enough oil to cover any food to be fried and still allow space for the oil to bubble up somewhat if moist food is added. For non-electric deep fryers, a deep-frying thermometer is a prerequisite. All the pieces of food to be deep-fried should be of the same size, to cook in the same amount of time without burning. A basket helps to lift a number of pieces at once and speeds up the process. There are several methods of preparing food for deep-frying: it can simply be dipped in flour, or it can be dipped in flour, then egg and finally rolled in bread crumbs. It can also be coated with an egg-and-flour batter or encased in pastry. Whatever method is used, observe a few basic rules: place the fryer on the back of the stove, heat the oil and fry a few pieces at a time so that the temperature of the oil is not lowered too drastically, and when the food has fried its alloted time, let it drain in single layers placed on a baking sheet lined with paper towels and set in a 250 F. warming oven. Serve fried foods on attractive paper liners that will absorb any residual oil. (**Note:** If the oil should flame up immediately cap the pot with a lid, *Never* throw water on the flames; it will turn to scalding steam. Cook with an open box of baking soda at your side to douse any flames.)

**Baked Appetizers.** These are always welcome! And the pastry can be baked blind (without a filling) way ahead of time. The great variety of tiny pastry shapes on the market, the little boat shapes called *barquettes*, and the many round and oval tartlet pans, are the sort of kitchenware the dedicated baker can never have too many of. Freeze, then unmold and stack the blind-baked pastry with paper between each one, wrap and return to the freezer. Before filling them, let them come to room temperature. For serving baked appetizers, whether *barquettes*, *filo*-wrapped *boeregs* or cheese straws, an electric hot tray is almost indispensable.

**Final Thoughts.** The serving and the eating of appetizers should take place in an atmosphere of relaxed bonhomie. The occasion should be fun for the cook as well as for the guests. If you have doubts about how elaborate to make it, follow one simple rule: Plan to be a guest at your own party, not a servant. Don't miss the fun.

# Dips, Spreads, Molds and Canapés

## RILLETTES (POTTED PORK)

**Mireille Johnston**

Mireille Johnston

2 to 3 cups

Most French provinces have their own special *rillettes*. Some are made with duck, others with rabbit, and still others with goose, but the one I like best of all is made with pork, vegetables and spices cooked slowly into a fragrant purée. The preparation, though time-consuming, is nonetheless easy, and the *rillettes* will keep for months.

1 POUND LEAN SALT PORK, CUT INTO
  3" PIECES
1 POUND PORK BELLY (FRESH BACON),
  CUT INTO 3" PIECES
1 POUND PORK SHOULDER, CUT INTO
  3" PIECES
3 CARROTS, PEELED
½ CUP CHOPPED SHALLOTS OR
  SCALLIONS

2 CLOVES GARLIC, PEELED AND
  CRUSHED
2 WHOLE CLOVES
3 BAY LEAVES
¼ CUP WATER
2 TABLESPOONS DRIED THYME
SALT, TO TASTE
FRESHLY GROUND WHITE PEPPER,
  TO TASTE

1. In a large, heavy-bottomed pan, combine all the pork (salt, belly and shoulder), the carrots, shallots (or scallions), garlic, cloves and bay leaves and add ¼ cup of water. Add the thyme, salt and pepper, cover, and cook for about 4 hours over low heat. Stir from time to time with a long wooden spoon, and add more water if the meat sticks to the pan.

2. Place a sturdy colander over a large bowl and pour the cooked meat and vegetable mixture into it. Press the solids gently with the back of a spoon to let most of the fat drain through into the bowl. Set the bowl of fat aside.

3. Transfer the solid mass of *rillettes* into a strong pan or big bowl and pound it energetically with a wooden pestle or heavy spoon.

   **Note:** Do not use either a blender or food processor for this step since they tend to destroy the fibrous texture of the *rillettes* and turn them into mush.

4. Check the seasoning. *Rillettes* should be highly seasoned.

5. Using two large forks, fluff up the mixture, return to the heat and cook for about 15 minutes, adding a little of the reserved, drained-off fat to make the mixture a little smoother.

6. Pack the warm spread into stoneware, earthenware, china or glass jars and

cover with a 1'' layer of the reserved fat. Cool completely. Cover each container with waxed paper or aluminum foil and tie with a decorative colored string or a rubber band. The *rillettes* will keep for months in a cool place.

**Note:** Use attractive, decorative pots or jars since the *rillettes* should be served directly from the container.

7. Serve with toasted whole wheat or rye bread, unsalted butter, little sour gherkins (*cornichons*) and a tart arugula salad.

---

# APPETIZER PIES

### Isabel S. Cornell

8 to 12 "pies"

The eye appeal of these fanciful canapés belies the ease and quickness of their preparation.

**Cream Cheese Spread:**
12 OUNCES CREAM CHEESE, SOFTENED
2 TABLESPOONS CREAM, MILK OR SOUR CREAM
½ ONION, GRATED
SALT, TO TASTE
PEPPER, TO TASTE
2 TABLESPOONS CHOPPED PIMIENTO
2 TABLESPOONS CHOPPED CHIVES
2 TABLESPOONS WELL-DRAINED PICKLE RELISH
1 TABLESPOON CHOPPED NUTS

**Egg Salad Spread:**
8 EGGS, HARD-COOKED
½ TEASPOON DRY MUSTARD
DASH OF CAYENNE PEPPER
⅓ CUP MINCED CELERY
MAYONNAISE
SALT, TO TASTE
PEPPER, TO TASTE

2 TABLESPOONS MINCED GREEN PEPPER
2 TO 3 TABLESPOONS GRATED SHARP CHEDDAR CHEESE
1 TABLESPOON MINCED CAPERS
2 TABLESPOONS MINCED OR DEVILLED HAM

**Other Ingredients:**
2 TO 3 ROUND LOAVES OF BREAD, ABOUT 10'' IN DIAMETER, SLICED *HORIZONTALLY* INTO ½''-THICK LAYERS (ASK THE STORE TO SLICE THE BREAD FOR YOU)
MAYONNAISE
VARIOUS GARNISHES: PAPRIKA, CHOPPED GREEN OR BLACK OLIVES, CHOPPED CHIVES OR PARSLEY, GRATED CARROTS, CHOPPED NUTS, MINCED GREEN PEPPERS, SALMON ROE, ETC.

1. Mash the cream cheese together with the cream (milk or sour cream), onion, salt and pepper.

2. Divide the mixture into four portions. Set one portion aside. Add the pimiento to one of the remaining three, the chives to the second, and the relish and nuts to the third. Cover all four portions and refrigerate until ready to use.

3. Peel the eggs and separate into yolks and whites.

4. Mash the egg yolks together with the mustard and cayenne. Finely chop the whites and combine them with the yolks and celery. Add enough mayonnaise to bind the mixture and season with salt and pepper.

---

Continued from preceding page

5. Divide the mixture into three parts. Set one part aside. Add the green pepper and grated cheddar to the second (plus more mayonnaise, if needed) and taste for seasoning. Add the capers and ham to the third portion. Cover all three portions and refrigerate until ready to use.

6. With sharp scissors, trim the crusts from the bread, using a plate or paper cut-out to make the slices as round and as large as possible. (The trimmed layers do not necessarily have to be of uniform size.) Cover the bread to keep it fresh while assembling the "pies."

7. Assemble several "pies" simultaneously. Spread the tops and sides of each slice of bread with a thin coating of mayonnaise.

8. Put a quarter-sized dab of the plain mixture (either egg or cream cheese) in the center of each slice. Surround this with a band of one of the flavored portions. Surround this band with a filling of contrasting flavor and color. Repeat until the entire slice is covered. Use different combinations for each "pie."

9. Dip the mayonnaise coated edge of the "pie" into one of the various garnishes to add color.

10. Chill until ready to serve. With scissors, cut each "pie" into 12 wedge-shaped portions.

# GUACAMOLE

## Paula J. Buchholz

2 cups

*Guacamole* lends itself to a wide variety of uses. It can be served as a filling for tacos or sandwiches, a topping for enchiladas, a dip with corn chips or deep-fried tortilla wedges, or it can be thinned out a bit with oil and vinegar and used as a salad dressing.

2 RIPE AVOCADOS, PEELED AND PITTED
2 TABLESPOONS FRESHLY SQUEEZED LEMON OR LIME JUICE
1 TABLESPOON MINCED ONION
1 CLOVE GARLIC, PEELED
½ TEASPOON CHILI POWDER

½ TEASPOON SALT
A FEW DROPS OF HOT RED PEPPER SAUCE
1 RIPE TOMATO, PEELED, SEEDED AND DICED (OPTIONAL)
½ CUP COOKED, CRUMBLED BACON (OPTIONAL)

1. In the container of a food processor or blender, process the avocados until smooth.

2. Add the lemon or lime juice, onion, garlic, chili powder, salt and pepper sauce, and continue processing for a few seconds longer, until the mixture is smoothly blended.

3. If desired, stir in either the tomato or bacon and serve.

# ASSORTED CANAPÉS

**Paul Rubinstein**

6 to 12 servings

### Egg and Anchovy Canapés:
2 TABLESPOONS OLIVE OIL
6 SLICES SANDWICH BREAD,
   CRUSTS TRIMMED
3 TABLESPOONS MAYONNAISE
2 TEASPOONS PREPARED MUSTARD
3 HARD-COOKED EGGS, THINLY
   SLICED
1 CAN (2 OUNCES) ANCHOVY FILLETS

1. In a skillet, heat the olive oil, add the bread, and fry on both sides until golden brown. Add more oil to the skillet if needed. Remove the bread from the pan and drain on paper towels.

2. In a small bowl, combine the mayonnaise and mustard.

3. Spread a thin coating of the mustard-flavored mayonnaise on the fried bread.

4. Arrange the sliced egg on the bread in a slightly overlapping pattern.

5. Cut each slice of toast diagonally in both directions to form four triangles.

6. Cut the anchovy fillets in half and place one piece across each triangle.

### Cucumber Canapés:
6 TABLESPOONS (¾ STICK) BUTTER,
   SOFTENED
1 TABLESPOON VERY FINELY
   CHOPPED FRESH PARSLEY
1 TABLESPOON VERY FINELY
   CHOPPED WATERCRESS
6 SLICES SANDWICH BREAD, CRUSTS
   REMOVED
1 LARGE OR 2 SMALL CUCUMBERS,
   UNPEELED AND THINLY SLICED
SALT, TO TASTE
FRESHLY GROUND BLACK PEPPER,
   TO TASTE

1. Combine the softened butter with the parsley and watercress and spread the mixture on the bread.

2. Arrange the cucumber slices on the buttered bread in an overlapping pattern. Sprinkle with salt and pepper.

3. With a sharp, heavy chef's knife, cut the canapés into triangles or rectangles and serve.

### Cheese and Apple Canapés:
6 SLICES SANDWICH BREAD,
   CRUSTS REMOVED
4 TABLESPOONS (½ STICK)
   BUTTER, SOFTENED
¼ POUND MILD CHEDDAR CHEESE,
   THINLY SLICED
2 TO 3 FRESH, FIRM EATING
   APPLES
1 LEMON

*Continued from preceding page*

1. Toast or grill the bread slices and spread them with the butter.

2. Arrange the sliced cheddar over the toast in a thin layer.

3. Peel, quarter and core the apples, and cut into thin crescent-shaped slices.

4. Cut the lemon in half, sprinkle the apple slices with lemon juice and toss together to prevent discoloration. Arrange the slices over the cheese in an overlapping patter.

5. Cut the toast into attractive shapes and serve.

### Smoked Salmon Canapés:

6 SLICES WHITE SANDWICH BREAD OR PUMPERNICKEL, CRUSTS TRIMMED
4 TABLESPOONS (½ STICK) UNSALTED BUTTER
¼ POUND THINLY SLICED SMOKED SALMON
JUICE OF ½ LEMON
FRESHLY GROUND BLACK PEPPER
4 HARD-COOKED EGG YOLKS
1 SMALL GHERKIN, THINLY SLICED

1. Toast the white bread. (Pumpernickel does not need to be toasted.)

2. Spread the bread with the butter.

3. Arrange the salmon in a thin layer over the butter. Sprinkle with the lemon juice and a grind of pepper.

4. Rub the egg yolks through a sieve and sprinkle over the salmon.

5. Cut the canapés into triangles or other suitable shapes. Decorate each individual canapé with a slice of the gherkin.

### Ham Canapés:

6 TABLESPOONS MAYONNAISE
2 TEASPOONS STRONG PREPARED MUSTARD
6 SLICES SANDWICH BREAD, CRUSTS TRIMMED
¼ POUND THINLY SLICED COOKED HAM
1 LARGE OR 2 SMALL JUST-RIPE TOMATOES, VERY THINLY SLICED
1 TEASPOON SALT
¼ TEASPOON FRESHLY GROUND BLACK PEPPER

1. In a small bowl, blend together the mayonnaise and mustard.

2. Spread the mixture on the bread.

3. Arrange the sliced ham over the spread in a thin layer.

4. Arrange the sliced tomato over the ham in an overlapping pattern.

5. Cut the bread into triangles or other shapes, sprinkle with the salt and pepper, and serve.

### Shrimp Canapés:

1 LEMON, QUARTERED
¼ POUND RAW SHRIMP, PEELED AND DEVEINED
6 TABLESPOONS MAYONNAISE
1 TABLESPOON FRESH, CHOPPED OR 1½ TEASPOONS DRIED DILL WEED
4 DROPS OF TABASCO SAUCE
6 SLICES SANDWICH BREAD, CRUSTS TRIMMED
3 PIMIENTOS, CUT INTO LONG, THIN STRIPS

1. Bring 2 quarts of water to a rolling boil. Squeeze the lemon quarters and drop

them into the water.

2. Add the shrimp and boil exactly 5 minutes. Drain the shrimp and allow them to cool. Slice each shrimp lengthwise into two or three thin slices.

3. In a small bowl, mix the mayonnaise with the chopped (or dried) dill weed and Tabasco.

4. Spread the seasoned mayonnaise on the sliced bread. Arrange the shrimp over the spread in a slightly overlapping pattern.

5. Cut the bread into various shapes and decorate each canapé with a strip of pimiento.

# TAPENADE

### Carol Cutler

2 cups

The name of this zesty spread comes from the old Provençal word for capers (*tapènes*), an important ingredient of the *tapenade*, a dish rarely found outside Provence, probably because of the traditionally laborious method of its preparation. Today, however, with the food processor, this has ceased to be a problem. The *tapenade* can also be made in a blender, though not as easily, and will require more oil with that method. Serve the *tapenade* spread on melba toast.

1½ CUPS OIL-CURED BLACK OLIVES (PREFERABLY GREEK OR FRENCH), PITTED
¼ TO ⅓ CUP OLIVE OIL
2 TABLESPOONS LEMON JUICE
2 TABLESPOONS BRANDY
1 CAN (3¼ OUNCES) TUNA FISH, IN OIL
1 BOTTLE (3¼ OUNCES) CAPERS, DRAINED
1 OUNCE ANCHOVY FILLETS, IN OIL

1 CLOVE GARLIC, PEELED AND CHOPPED
1½ TABLESPOONS ENGLISH MUSTARD POWDER
½ TEASPOON FINELY GROUND BLACK PEPPER
LARGE PINCH OF GROUND CLOVES
LARGE PINCH OF GROUND GINGER
LARGE PINCH OF FRESHLY GRATED NUTMEG

1. Put the olives into the container of a food processor, with the steel knife in place.

2. With the motor running, pour ¼ cup of the olive oil into the container.

3. Turn off the motor and add the remaining ingredients.

4. Process the mixture to a smooth paste. Add the remaining oil if desired.

5. Taste and correct the seasoning if necessary. Scrape the paste into a container, cover and refrigerate.

**Note:** If an electric blender is used, combine the oil, lemon juice and brandy before slowly adding the remaining ingredients. Some blenders may require more oil than indicated above. *Tapenade* keeps well under refrigeration and can also be frozen.

# ANCHOVY AND GARLIC SPREAD (ANCHOÏADES)

## Mireille Johnston

6 servings

*Anchoïades* are spicy anchovy and garlic spreads generally served on dry toast. The first of these two *anchoïade* recipes is a powerful, concentrated version, to be served hot; the second is creamy and is served cold.

*Anchoïade* I:
20 ANCHOVY FILLETS (PREFERABLY
    PACKED IN COARSE SALT)
2 CLOVES GARLIC, CRUSHED
1 TABLESPOON RED WINE VINEGAR
    OR LEMON JUICE
FRESHLY GROUND BLACK PEPPER,
    TO TASTE
¼ CUP OLIVE OIL, APPROXIMATELY
6 SLICES GOOD WHITE BREAD OR 12
    SLICES FRENCH BREAD

Garnishes (Optional):
CRUSHED GARLIC
LEMON SLICES
RADISHES
CHOPPED PARSLEY OR CHIVES
BLACK OLIVES

1. Mash the anchovies in a mortar, or use a blender or food processor.

2. Add the garlic, vinegar (or lemon juice) and pepper. Continuing to mash or process, dribble the ¼ cup of oil in very slowly so the sauce does not separate.

3. Sprinkle the bread slices with some olive oil, place on a cookie sheet, and toast under the broiler for 2 to 3 minutes, or until slightly crisp.

4. Turn the slices over, spread them with the anchovy paste, and return to the broiler for 3 to 5 minutes.

5. Cut each slice into four triangles and serve piping hot. If desired, sprinkle the triangles with crushed garlic and arrange them on a platter with lemon slices, white or red radishes, chopped parsley or chives, and black olives.

*Anchoïade* II:
24 ANCHOVY FILLETS (PREFERABLY
    PACKED IN COARSE SALT)
2 CLOVES GARLIC, PEELED
2 EGG YOLKS
¼ CUP OLIVE OIL, APPROXIMATELY
FRESHLY GROUND BLACK PEPPER,
    TO TASTE
6 SLICES GOOD WHITE BREAD

Garnishes (Optional):
CHOPPED PARSLEY OR CHIVES
1 HARD-COOKED EGG, PASSED
    THROUGH A SIEVE
1 ONION, GRATED
SMALL BLACK OLIVES
SLICED RADISHES

1. Mash the anchovies and garlic in a mortar.

2. Add the egg yolks and mix well.

3. Very slowly beat in the ¼ cup of oil, then add the pepper.

4. Sprinkle the bread slices with some olive oil and toast lightly under the broiler for 2 to 3 minutes.

5. Cut the bread into triangles while still hot; let them cool and then spread with the anchovy paste.

6. If desired, top with any of the suggested garnishes.

# VELVET EGGS WITH CAVIAR

**Marion Lear Swaybill**

6 to 8 servings

I received a food processor as a birthday gift. It was a Sunday, I had not planned to cook and my cupboard was relatively bare. The only thing I had on hand to try in my new treasure were some hard-cooked eggs. After some improvising I came up with this recipe. Serve the eggs very cold, with thinly sliced black or rye bread, crackers or cucumber slices.

8 HARD-COOKED EGGS, QUARTERED
½ TEASPOON SALT
¼ TEASPOON FRESHLY GROUND
   WHITE PEPPER
¾ CUP MAYONNAISE
1 JAR (3½ OUNCES) RED OR BLACK
   LUMPFISH CAVIAR

1. In a food processor or blender, combine the eggs, salt and pepper and process until the eggs are finely chopped.

2. Add the mayonnaise, ¼ cup at a time, and continue processing.

   **Note:** The eggs may acquire the desired taste and/or consistency with less than the ¾ cup mayonnaise indicated. Taste is a big factor here.

3. Mound the processed mixture on a serving plate and surround it with the caviar. Serve very cold with thinly sliced black or rye bread, crackers or cucumber slices.

# HUMMUS BI TAHINI
# (CHICK-PEA DIP WITH SESAME PASTE)

**Michael Batterberry**

About 6 cups

4 CUPS COOKED OR CANNED CHICK-
   PEAS
¼ CUP COLD WATER
¼ CUP PEANUT OIL
1 CUP *TAHINI* (SESAME PASTE, AVAIL-
   ABLE IN SPECIALTY MARKETS)
1½ TEASPOONS GROUND CUMIN
JUICE OF 2 OR MORE LIMES, ACCORD-
   ING TO TASTE

2 DASHES OF TABASCO SAUCE
2 TO 4 CLOVES GARLIC, CRUSHED
1¼ TEASPOONS KOSHER SALT
½ TO ¾ CUPS ROASTED, SKINNED
   SWEET RED PEPPERS IN OLIVE OIL
   (OPTIONAL)

1. Purée all of the ingredients in a food processor or blender until light and fluffy.

   **Note:** If a blender is used, the ingredients will probably have to be divided into two or three separate batches.

2. Scrape into a decorative bowl and, if desired, garnish with strips of sweet red peppers.

3. Serve with warm or toasted *pita* bread.

# AÏOLI MÉNAGÈRE

**Robert Renaud**

2 cups

The addition of a boiled potato to the traditional classic ingredients of the *aïoli ménagère*—home-style garlic-flavored mayonnaise—imparts a marvelous texture to the sauce. It can be most successfully achieved if all the ingredients are at room temperature.

4 LARGE CLOVES (1 OUNCE) GARLIC,
   PEELED
1 MEDIUM-SIZED BAKING POTATO,
   BOILED, PEELED AND BROKEN UP
   WITH A FORK
1 EGG YOLK
PINCH OF SALT
½ CUP OLIVE OIL
LEMON JUICE
COLD WATER

1. With a mortar and pestle, mash the garlic into a paste.

2. Add the potato and blend in thoroughly.

3. Blend in the egg yolk and salt, and then add the olive oil in a slow, steady stream, beating very rapidly all the while, and squeezing in a little lemon juice from time to time.

4. After all the oil has been beaten in, beat in a little cold water to keep the sauce from separating. (If by chance it should separate, add another egg yolk.)

5. Serve the *aïoli* with any white fish cooked in a court-bouillon, or with cold meats, hard-cooked eggs, or boiled, steamed or raw vegetables.


# ECONOMICAL PARTY PÂTÉ

**Jane Moulton**

12 servings

8 TABLESPOONS (1 STICK) BUTTER OR
   MARGARINE
2 MEDIUM-SIZED ONIONS, CUT INTO
   CHUNKS
1 CLOVE GARLIC, PEELED
1 POUND BEEF LIVER, WITH SINEWY
   STRIPS REMOVED

½ TEASPOON SALT
1 TEASPOON UNFLAVORED GELATIN
⅔ CUP WATER
1 TEASPOON INSTANT BEEF
   BOUILLON
¼ CUP DRY SHERRY

1. In a large skillet, melt the butter or margarine. Add the onions, garlic and liver, and sauté over high heat until the meat is cooked through but still pink inside.

2. While the meat is cooking, cut it into pieces small enough to be ground in a food processor or blender, and sprinkle with the salt.

3. Transfer the mixture to a bowl and return the skillet to the stove.

4. Soak the gelatin in 2 tablespoons of water for 10 minutes. Then add the gelatin, beef bouillon and ½ cup of the water to the skillet. Turn up the heat and stir to scrape all the browned bits from the bottom of the pan and to dissolve the gelatin.

5. Now purée the liver mixture in two batches in a blender or all at once in a food processor. If using a blender, add half of this bouillon mixture to each batch of the meat mixture, along with half of the sherry. If using a food processor, purée the meat mixture, then add the bouillon and the sherry and process just to combine.

6. Pour into a 3-cup mold or into three 1-cup soufflé dishes. Chill for at least 4 hours or overnight.

# TABBOULEH

## Paula J. Buchholz

4 servings

A tart hors d'oeuvre, vegetable course or salad, this lemony variation of a traditional Middle Eastern appetizer is perfect for picnics or informal suppers. It is one salad that won't wilt no matter how long it sits on the buffet table.

½ CUP FINE BULGUR (TOASTED, CRUSHED WHEAT AVAILABLE IN SPECIALTY AND HEALTH FOOD STORES)
¾ CUP FRESHLY SQUEEZED LEMON JUICE
2 CUPS DICED TOMATOES
1½ CUPS FINELY CHOPPED FRESH PARSLEY
1 CUP FINELY CHOPPED GREEN ONIONS
1 CUP DICED CUCUMBER
½ CUP FINELY CHOPPED FRESH MINT
⅓ CUP FRUITY OLIVE OIL
SALT, TO TASTE
FRESHLY GROUND BLACK PEPPER, TO TASTE
ROMAINE LETTUCE LEAVES OR *PITA* BREAD

1. In a bowl, combine the crushed wheat with enough cold water to cover it completely. Soak the wheat for about 10 minutes and then drain well.

   **Note:** The grain should be completely dry before it is combined with the other ingredients.

2. In a deep bowl, combine the well-drained wheat with the lemon juice, tomatoes, parsley, green onions, cucumber, mint and olive oil. Toss gently but thoroughly with a fork. Season with the salt and pepper.

3. To serve, mound the *tabbouleh* in a bowl and scoop up with romaine lettuce leaves or pieces of *pita* bread.

# RUSSIAN EGGPLANT APPETIZER

**Ruth Spear**

4 to 6 cups

VEGETABLE OIL
3 LARGE ONIONS, COARSELY CHOP-
  PED
3 CLOVES GARLIC, MINCED
2 LARGE EGGPLANTS
2 GREEN PEPPERS
4 TO 6 CARROTS

2 CUPS TOMATO KETCHUP
SALT
FRESHLY GROUND BLACK PEPPER
SUGAR
CAYENNE PEPPER
½ CUP MINCED PARSLEY
CHOPPED FRESH DILL

1. In a large, heavy pot, heat an appropriate amount of oil and sauté the onions until soft. Add the garlic and continue cooking until the garlic is pale gold.

2. While the onions and garlic are cooking, prepare the vegetables. Remove the stem and blossom ends of the eggplant and cut it (unpeeled) into 1'' cubes. Seed the peppers and cut them into 1'' pieces. Scrape the carrots and cut them into 1'' pieces.

3. Add the green pepper and carrots to the onions, and sauté until lightly browned, adding more oil if necessary. Stir frequently and add a little water to keep them from sticking.

4. Add the eggplant, cover and cook on very low heat for 1½ hours. Stir frequently and add oil and/or water as needed to keep the bottom from scorching.

5. When the vegetables are very soft, uncover and cook until excess liquid has evaporated. Stir in the ketchup.

6. Season to taste with salt, pepper, sugar and a dash or two of cayenne. Stir in the parsley and dill and cook gently for 10 minutes.

7. Cool and refrigerate.

8. Serve in a bowl for spreading, with brown or black bread.

**Note:** This dip may be frozen until needed, but let it come to room temperature before serving.

# TARAMASALATA

**Emanuel and Madeline Greenberg**

About 1¼ cups

Sometimes referred to as a caviar spread, this Greek appetizer is actually made with salted carp roe. An indispensible part of any assortment of hors d'oeuvres in Greek homes or restaurants, it can be served either as a spread or a dip with *pita* bread, crusty French or Italian loaves or sesame crackers. In Greece it is accompanied with ouzo (a potent, anise-flavored aperitif) either chilled or on the rocks, taken straight or with a splash of cold water.

2 SLICES FIRM WHITE BREAD,
   CRUSTS TRIMMED
COLD WATER
¼ CUP *TARAMA* (CARP ROE)*
JUICE OF 1 LEMON (SCANT ¼ CUP)
½ CUP OLIVE OIL
2 TABLESPOONS CHOPPED ONION
DASH OF GARLIC POWDER
ITALIAN FLAT-LEAF PARSLEY,
   CHOPPED

1. Soak the bread briefly in cold water and squeeze dry.

2. In the container of a blender or food processor, combine the bread with the *tarama*, lemon juice, 2 tablespoons of the olive oil, the onion and garlic powder. Process and gradually add the remaining oil, until the mixture takes on the consistency of mayonnaise. Chill.

3. Garnish with the parsley and serve.

* *Tarama* is available both loose and in jars in Greek food stores. The packaged roe is sometimes also found in well-stocked delicatessens. The loose variety is to be preferred if you can get it.

## YOGURT CHEESE WITH SCALLIONS AND WALNUTS

Michael Batterberry

1 quart

8 CUPS PLAIN YOGURT
¾ CUP FINELY MINCED SCALLIONS
2 CUPS COARSELY CHOPPED
   WALNUTS
1 TEASPOON KOSHER SALT
FRESHLY GROUND BLACK PEPPER,
   TO TASTE
SLIVERED BLACK OLIVES

1. Line a colander with several layers of well-rinsed cheesecloth, letting enough of the cheesecloth hang over the edges to fold back over the surface of the yogurt.

2. Place the yogurt in the colander, cover with the excess cloth, set the colander in a bowl and refrigerate it overnight. The volume of the yogurt should reduce by half.

3. Before serving, if you discover that the yogurt has become overly reduced, beat in a little of the liquid which drained off onto the bowl. Stir in the scallions, walnuts, salt and freshly ground black pepper.

4. Pile the mixture decoratively into a pedestal dish or bowl and decorate the top with slivers of black olives. Serve with toasted *pita* bread (or, if you like, you could stuff celery or endive spears with the mixture).

# LOBSTER MOUSSE WITH CUCUMBER SAUCE

**Marion Lear Swaybill**

6 servings

1 TABLESPOON UNFLAVORED GELATIN
¼ CUP COLD WATER
3 TABLESPOONS LEMON JUICE
¾ CUP MAYONNAISE, OR ¼ CUP SOUR
  CREAM AND ½ CUP MAYONNAISE
1 CUP FINELY MINCED CELERY
1½ CUPS MINCED, COOKED LOB-
  STER MEAT
2 TEASPOONS GRATED ONION

½ CUP HEAVY CREAM, WHIPPED
SALT, TO TASTE
FRESHLY GROUND PEPPER, TO TASTE

Cucumber Sauce:
1 PACKAGE (8 OUNCES) CREAM
  CHEESE
½ CUP LIGHT CREAM
1 CUP MINCED CUCUMBER

1. In a heatproof bowl, soften the gelatin in the cold water. Set the bowl in a pan of simmering water, and stir until the crystals dissolve.

2. Add the gelatin and lemon juice to the mayonnaise and blend.

3. In the container of a blender or food processor, combine the celery, lobster meat and onion and process until smooth and homogenized.

4. Fold the lobster mixture into the mayonnaise.

5. Fold the whipped cream into the lobster-mayonnaise mixture. Season with salt and pepper.

6. Spoon the mousse into a 1-quart mold and chill overnight.

7. Before serving the mousse, make the cucumber sauce. Soften the cream cheese and blend in the light cream.

8. Add the minced cucumber and stir well.

9. Unmold the mousse, garnish with watercress, Italian parsley or other fresh greens, and serve with the cucumber sauce on the side.


# SAVORY RELISH MOLDS

**Isabel S. Cornell**

12 to 15 slices each

Little do-it-yourself sandwiches are perfect finger food for the cocktail buffet. Cut these savory gelatin molds into thin slices and serve with a variety of thinly sliced cooked meats (baked ham, roast beef, lean corned beef, meat loaf, tongue, chicken loaf, roast turkey breast, etc.) and thin slices of bread (white, rye, French, sourdough, whole wheat, seeded, cheese, egg, etc.), cut to the size of the meat slices. Each guest can then choose a relish slice, meat slice and bread that are compatible to create any number of different taste combinations. The main advantage to these savory molds is that they are easy to serve, won't drip and don't have to be spread.

**Jellied Horseradish Slices:**
1 ENVELOPE UNFLAVORED GELATIN
¼ CUP WATER
½ CUP BOILING-HOT BEEF
    BOUILLON
1 TO 2 TABLESPOONS PREPARED
    HORSERADISH
1 TEASPOON LEMON JUICE
¼ CUP SOUR CREAM
¼ CUP MAYONNAISE
SALT, TO TASTE
PEPPER, TO TASTE
SNIPPED FRESH CHIVES

1. Soak the gelatin in ¼ cup of water and stir it into the boiling bouillon until the gelatin dissolves. Cool to room temperature.

2. Combine the horseradish, lemon juice, sour cream and mayonnaise. Add this to the gelatin, and season with salt and pepper.

3. Turn the mixture into a 1½-cup oiled mold and chill until firm.

4. Unmold, slice and sprinkle with the snipped chives.

**Savory Mustard Slices:**
1 ENVELOPE UNFLAVORED GELATIN
¼ CUP WATER
½ CUP BOILING-HOT CHICKEN
    CONSOMMÉ
1 TEASPOON DRY MUSTARD
1 TO 2 TABLESPOONS PREPARED
    YELLOW MUSTARD
½ CUP MAYONNAISE
MINCED FRESH PARSLEY

1. Soak the gelatin in ¼ cup of water and stir it into the boiling consommé until the gelatin dissolves. Add the dry mustard and cool to room temperature.

2. Mix the prepared mustard with the mayonnaise and beat it into the broth.

3. Turn the mixture into a 1½-cup oiled mold and chill until firm.

4. Unmold, slice and garnish with the minced parsley.

# HAM MOUSSE

**Florence Fabricant**

About 6 cups

¼ CUP CHOPPED ONION
1 TABLESPOON BUTTER
1½ CUPS CHICKEN BROTH
2 ENVELOPES UNFLAVORED GELATIN
⅓ CUP DRY WHITE WINE
2 CUPS CHOPPED BOILED HAM
½ CUP MINCED *PROSCIUTTO*
1 TABLESPOON DIJON-STYLE MUS-
    TARD
PINCH OF CAYENNE PEPPER
¼ TEASPOON THYME
1 CUP HEAVY CREAM
2 TABLESPOONS BRANDY
2 TABLESPOONS MINCED PARSLEY
1 TO 2 TABLESPOONS TOMATO PASTE
    (OPTIONAL)

1. In a saucepan, sauté the onion in the butter until soft. Add the chicken broth and simmer gently.

*Continued from preceding page*

2. Meanwhile, soften the gelatin in the wine. Add it to the saucepan, stirring to dissolve the gelatin.

3. Place the ham and *prosciutto* in a blender jar or food processor. Add the broth mixture along with the mustard, cayenne and thyme and process to a fine purée. Taste carefully for seasoning. Chill the mixture until it is just beginning to set.

4. Whip the cream until it forms soft peaks, then gently but thoroughly fold it into the chilled ham mixture.

5. Stir in the brandy, parsley and, if necessary for color, tomato paste.

6. Spoon the mousse into a 6-cup mold and chill for at least 2 hours.

7. To serve, dip the mold in hot water, hold a plate upside down over it and quickly invert the mold so the mousse slips onto the plate. Liberally dust the mousse with some minced parsley and serve it with fresh melba toast.

**Note:** For a more elaborate presentation, the mousse may be chilled in an 8-cup mold that has been lined with a clear white wine aspic set with hard-cooked egg slices, truffles or other decorations.

# CHEESE MOUSSE

**Carol Cutler**

18 servings

1½ CUPS BEEF BROTH
2 TABLESPOONS (2 ENVELOPES) UN-
  FLAVORED GELATIN
½ TO 1 CLOVE GARLIC, SLICED
¼ TEASPOON CURRY POWDER
½ TEASPOON WORCESTERSHIRE
  SAUCE
DASH OF TABASCO SAUCE
SALT, TO TASTE
PEPPER, TO TASTE
12 OUNCES (1½ PACKAGES) CREAM
  CHEESE
LETTUCE LEAVES
BLACK OLIVES

1. Pour the broth into a small saucepan, sprinkle the gelatin over it, and let stand for a few minutes. Set the pot over medium heat to soften the gelatin. Allow the broth to become quite hot, but do not let it boil. Stir a few times to dissolve the gelatin completely. Remove from the heat and let cool.

2. Pour the cooled broth into a blender. Add the garlic, curry powder, Worcestershire and Tabasco sauces, salt and pepper. Blend for 30 seconds.

3. With the blender running, add about one-third of the cream cheese at a time. When all of the cheese is incorporated, give the mixture one final burst of high speed.

4. Pour the mixture into a 3-cup mold and refrigerate for about 3 hours, or until the mousse is set.

5. To unmold, cut around the edges of the mousse with a hot knife, then dip the bottom of the mold in hot water for a few seconds. Unmold onto a bed of lettuce and decorate with black olives.

# Baked Pastries

## MUSSEL, HAM AND MUSHROOM PUFFS

Paula Wolfert

8 servings

Pastry Dough:
2 CUPS FLOUR
¾ TEASPOON SALT
8 TABLESPOONS (1 STICK) BUTTER
3 TABLESPOONS LARD
ICE WATER
1 EGG YOLK, BEATEN WITH 1 TEA-
SPOON WATER

Filling:
1 CAN (4 OUNCES) IMPORTED MUS-
SELS COOKED IN BUTTER
2 TABLESPOONS FINELY CHOPPED
VIRGINIA HAM

2 TABLESPOONS FINELY CHOPPED
MUSHROOMS
1 TEASPOON FINELY CHOPPED
GARLIC
SALT, TO TASTE
FRESHLY GROUND BLACK PEPPER,
TO TASTE
5 TABLESPOONS UNSALTED BUTTER
1 TABLESPOON FINELY CHOPPED
PARSLEY

1. Sift the flour and salt together into a bowl.

2. Blend in the butter and lard until the mixture resembles coarse oatmeal, with a few buttery lumps still visible.

3. Sprinkle a little ice water over the mixture, just enough so that it can be gathered into a ball. Wrap the dough in waxed paper and refrigerate for at least 30 minutes.

4. Drain the mussels and set aside.

5. Combine the ham, mushrooms, garlic, salt, pepper, butter and parsley, and mix well to a pastelike consistency.

6. Roll out the chilled dough into a long rectangle. Fold the rectangle into thirds. Give the dough a quarter turn and roll it into a long rectangle again. Fold it in thirds again, turn it and then roll it out to ¹/₈'' thickness. Cut into 2'' squares.

7. Put one mussel and a very small amount of the prepared ham-mushroom mixture in the center of each pastry square. Moisten the edges with water, gather the four corners up over the filling and pinch to seal them together.

Note: This much of the recipe can be prepared in advance and then chilled (but not frozen) until ready to bake.

*Continued from preceding page*

8. Preheat the oven to 350 F.

9. Arrange the filled puffs on an ungreased baking sheet about 1'' apart, prick them, and swab each with the egg wash.

10. Bake for 25 minutes and serve warm.

## INDIVIDUAL TOMATO AND CHEESE PIZZAS

### Paul Rubinstein

6 to 12 servings

This recipe is for six individual 5'' pizzas, a suitable portion for a first course. To serve as appetizers, cut each pizza into six wedges.

1½ PACKAGES ACTIVE DRY YEAST
1¼ CUPS LUKEWARM MILK
¾ TEASPOON SUGAR
4 CUPS ALL-PURPOSE FLOUR
1 TEASPOON SALT
6 TABLESPOONS OLIVE OIL
⅓ CUP CHOPPED ONION
1 SMALL CLOVE GARLIC, CRUSHED
   THROUGH A PRESS

2½ CUPS CANNED ITALIAN PLUM
   TOMATOES, DRAINED
¼ CUP THICK TOMATO PASTE
¼ TEASPOON FRESHLY GROUND
   BLACK PEPPER
½ POUND THINLY SLICED MOZZA-
   RELLA CHEESE

1. In a cup, mix the yeast with the milk and sugar and let it stand a few minutes, until it has dissolved completely and begun to bubble.

2. Place the yeast mixture in a bowl and sift in the flour together with ¾ teaspoon of the salt.

3. Stir to combine, then gather the dough into a mass and knead it either on a lightly floured board or using the dough hook attachment of an electric mixer. Knead until the dough is smooth and shiny. Cover with a damp towel and allow the dough to rise until it has approximately doubled in size.

4. Sprinkle the dough with a little flour and punch it down to deflate it. Cover again and let it rise 1 hour.

5. Meanwhile, make the sauce. In a saucepan, heat the olive oil. Add the onion and garlic to the pan and stir over medium heat until the onions soften and become translucent, but not brown. Add the tomatoes, tomato paste, the remaining ¼ teaspoon salt and the pepper. Stir the ingredients together and cook for a few minutes, until the tomatoes lose their shape and melt into the sauce. Turn off the heat and let the sauce cool.

6. Preheat the oven to 425 F.

7. Roll out the dough into a sheet about ¼'' thick. Cut out six 5'' circles. If necessary, cut out four or five circles the first time, then gather the scraps, roll the dough out again and cut out as many more circles as needed. Lay the circles of dough on cookie sheets.

8. Spread the tomato sauce in equal portions over the rounds of dough. Cover each

with a single layer of sliced mozzarella. Bake in the preheated oven about 30 minutes, or until the cheese melts and the edges of the crust are golden brown. Serve as is, or cut the rounds into wedges.

**Note:** If you want to prepare these pizzas somewhat in advance of serving, you may take them out of the oven when the crust has colored slightly. Leave the oven hot, then re-bake the pizzas for the few minutes still needed before serving.

## BOEREGS (ARMENIAN STUFFED PASTRIES)

Paula J. Buchholz

4 dozen pastries

1 POUND GROUND LAMB
1 ONION, FINELY MINCED
1 GREEN PEPPER, FINELY MINCED
2 TABLESPOONS CHOPPED FRESH
  PARSLEY
1 TABLESPOON CHOPPED FRESH
  BASIL, OR DRIED BASIL, TO TASTE

SALT, TO TASTE
FRESHLY GROUND BLACK PEPPER
½ CUP PINE NUTS OR SLIVERED
  ALMONDS
¾ POUND *FILO* DOUGH
½ POUND (2 STICKS) BUTTER, MELTED

1. Preheat the oven to 325 F.

2. Sauté the lamb, onion and green pepper until the lamb takes on color and the vegetables are soft.

3. Add the parsley, basil and salt. Season with a fair amount of pepper; the mixture should be somewhat peppery. Add the pine nuts (or almonds) and set aside to cool.

4. Unroll the *filo* dough and place it under a slightly damp kitchen towel to prevent it from drying out. Remove one sheet of *filo*, lay it on a work surface and brush it with melted butter. With a sharp knife, cut the *filo* lengthwise, into four 2''-wide strips.

   **Note:** There are a few tricks to handling the delicate *filo* pastry. Work away from sunlight and heat. *Filo* dries out quickly, and when it does, it becomes too brittle to be shaped. Keep any leaves you are not using covered with a slightly damp, not wet, cloth, or wrap and refrigerate.

5. Place a heaping teaspoonful of filling on one end of the pastry strip and fold over one corner to form a triangle. Continue folding the pastry from side to side in the shape of a triangle (as you would fold a flag), until all the dough is folded over the filling.

6. Repeat this process strip by strip, until all the filling has been used.

7. Place the *boeregs* on a buttered baking sheet and bake in the preheated oven for about 20 minutes, or until golden brown, and serve hot.

**Note:** Either baked or unbaked, these savory appetizers freeze beautifully.

# HERB AND BACON TARTLETS

**Susan Lipke**

16 tartlets

Pastry:
1 EGG YOLK
5 TO 7 TABLESPOONS ICE WATER
8 OUNCES (ABOUT 1¾ CUPS) FLOUR
1 TEASPOON SALT
PINCH OF SUGAR
10 TABLESPOONS (1¼ STICKS) WELL-CHILLED, UNSALTED BUTTER, CUT INTO SMALL PIECES
2 TABLESPOONS WELL-CHILLED SHORTENING, CUT INTO SEVERAL PIECES

Filling:
4 STRIPS BACON

3 TABLESPOONS BUTTER, APPROXIMATELY
2 TABLESPOONS FLOUR
1 CUP BOILING MILK
½ TEASPOON SALT
FRESHLY GROUND PEPPER, TO TASTE
PINCH OF CAYENNE PEPPER
FRESHLY GRATED NUTMEG
2 EGG YOLKS
½ CUP CHOPPED FRESH HERBS (TARRAGON, CHIVES, BASIL, PARSLEY)*
2 TO 3 TABLESPOONS GRATED GRUYÈRE CHEESE

1. In a cup or small bowl, beat the egg yolk with 5 tablespoons of ice water and set it next to your work surface.

2. In a bowl, toss together the flour, salt and sugar. Add the butter and shortening and cut it in rapidly, until all butter bits are pea-sized.

3. Stir the egg yolk-water mixture once, then pour it into the center of the flour-butter mixture. Stir together with a fork until all the liquid has been incorporated and all the flour moistened. If the mixture appears too dry, dribble in a little more ice water.

4. Gather the dough into a ball, place it on a pastry board and quickly rub egg-sized lumps away from you with the heel of the hand. Gather the pastry back into a ball, sprinkle with flour, wrap in plastic wrap and refrigerate for at least 2 hours.

5. Butter 16 individual tartlet tins, each approximately 2¾" across x ½" deep. (If you prefer, you can substitute two 8-unit tartlet frames, photo page 8.)

6. On a lightly floured work surface, roll out the dough to a thickness of ⅛". Cut it into 16 rounds about 3½" in diameter. Press the rounds into the tartlet forms, prick each with a fork and flute the edges. Refrigerate for 30 minutes.

   **Note:** The pastry recipe can be cut down if you wish to gather up the scraps and reroll them. I find this something of a bother, and prefer to freeze the scraps for future use.

7. Preheat the oven to 400 F.

8. Line the tartlet shells with rounds of parchment or waxed paper and weight them with beans. Bake in the preheated oven for 7 minutes, until they begin to set. Remove the paper and beans, prick again and bake 1 to 2 minutes longer, until they are set but before they take on color. Remove from the tins and cool on a wire rack.

9. Turn the oven down to 375 F.

10. While the tart shells are cooling, prepare the filling. Fry the bacon until crisp. Drain on paper towels and chop into ¼" pieces. Reserve.

11. In a small saucepan, melt 2 tablespoons of the butter over medium-low heat and stir in the flour. Cook, stirring constantly, for 2 minutes.

12. Remove from the heat and add the boiling milk, all at once, whisking until smooth. Add the salt, pepper, cayenne and several grinds of nutmeg; whisk in.

13. Return the pan to the heat and boil the mixture for 1 minute, stirring constantly. Remove from the heat and beat in the egg yolks.

14. Allow the sauce to cool a little, then stir in the chopped herbs and bacon.

15. Place the tartlet shells on a baking sheet and divide the filling among them. Sprinkle each with a little cheese and dot with the remaining butter.

16. Bake the tartlets in the preheated oven for 12 to 15 minutes, until puffed and lightly browned.

**Note:** You can substitute 4 large mushrooms (about 6 to 8 ounces) for the bacon. Dice and sauté them in about 1 tablespoon of butter; salt lightly.

* Try to use at least two of the suggested herbs; all four together are great. Do *not* substitute dried herbs.

---

# ARAB PIZZA

Paula Wolfert

16 pies

These open tartlets filled with a mixture of ground lamb or beef and onion, pine nuts, yogurt and spices make a delightful hors d'oeuvre. Traditionally they are made with a yeast dough which I find a little too heavy to serve with drinks. My variation uses a lighter cream cheese pastry.

**Cream Cheese Pastry:**
8 TABLESPOONS (1 STICK) UNSALTED BUTTER
⅔ CUP (5½ OUNCES) CREAM CHEESE
2 CUPS ALL-PURPOSE FLOUR
1 TEASPOON SALT

**Filling:**
2 TABLESPOONS BUTTER
½ CUP FINELY CHOPPED ONION
1 POUND GROUND LAMB OR BEEF

SALT, TO TASTE
FRESHLY GROUND BLACK PEPPER, TO TASTE
PINCH OF GROUND CLOVES
PINCH OF CINNAMON
PINCH OF GRATED NUTMEG
2 TABLESPOONS CHOPPED PARSLEY
⅓ CUP PINE NUTS, TOASTED IN THE OVEN
½ CUP PLAIN YOGURT

1. Blend the butter and the cream cheese together.

2. Work in the flour and the salt, and knead the dough to incorporate the flour evenly.

3. Wrap in waxed paper and chill for 2 hours.

*Continued from preceding page*

4. Preheat the oven to 350 F.

5. Roll out the dough between sheets of waxed paper and cut out sixteen 2½'' rounds. Form the dough circles into mini tart shells by turning up the edges to make small rims. With a spatula, move the tart shells to a baking sheet.

6. In a skillet, melt the butter, add the onion, and cook until soft but not brown.

7. Add the meat and continue cooking 3 to 4 minutes, breaking up any lumps of meat with a fork.

8. Add the salt, pepper and spices.

9. Mix in the parsley and the toasted pine nuts.

10. Allow to cool completely, then stir in the yogurt.

11. Fill the pastry tartlets and bake in the preheated oven for 30 minutes. Serve hot.

# CHEESE-STUFFED TRIANGLES AND SNAILS (TYROPITAKIA)

## Vilma Liacouras Chantiles

About 10 dozen

¾ POUND *FETA* CHEESE, APPROXI-
MATELY
1 POUND RICOTTA CHEESE
SALT, IF NECESSARY
2 TABLESPOONS CHOPPED FRESH
MINT OR DILL, OR ¼ TO ½ TEA-
SPOON FRESHLY GRATED NUTMEG

3 LARGE OR 4 MEDIUM-SIZED EGGS,
LIGHTLY BEATEN
½ POUND (2 STICKS) MARGARINE OR
BUTTER
1 POUND *FILO* PASTRY LEAVES

1. Crumble the ¾ pound of *feta* into a bowl. Add the ricotta and taste. The *feta* should dominate the flavors; if it doesn't, add more.

2. Taste the mixture again, this time for salt. If the *feta* you are using is very salty, do not add salt to the cheeses.

3. Add the mint, dill or nutmeg. Check the seasoning and add more if desired.

   **Note:** This much of the recipe can be prepared ahead of time. Cover the cheese mixture and refrigerate. Remove from the refrigerator 1 hour before assembling the *tyropitakia.*

4. Add the beaten eggs to the cheese mixture and stir well. Set aside while preparing the *filo.*

5. Melt the margarine (or butter) and keep it warm.

6. Count the *filo* pastry leaves (usually 20 to 24 leaves are available in each pound) and divide them in half. Reroll one of the two stacks, wrap it in waxed paper and then in a dampened dish towel, and place in the refrigerator.

7. Reroll the other stack of *filo* leaves, then, with a very sharp knife, cut the *filo* roll crosswise into six 2''-long segments (as you would slice French bread). These strips will be used to make the triangles.

8. Unroll the *filo* strips and stack them up. Cover with waxed paper and then a dampened kitchen towel to keep them from drying out (which they will do with surprising speed).

9. Lay one strip of *filo* on the working surface, short end toward you. Using a very soft pastry brush, spread the *filo* with the warm margarine or butter.

10. Place 1 teaspoon of the cheese filling 1'' in from the end of the *filo* nearest you, and slightly to the left of center. Lift the righthand corner of the *filo* and fold the pastry diagonally over the cheese, aligning the entire short end of the *filo* strip with the long lefthand side, thus forming a triangle.

11. Using whichever side of the triangle is uppermost as a guide for each turn, flop the cheese package over and over, until you reach the end of the *filo* strip.

    **Note:** This is the same folding pattern used for a flag.

12. Set the triangle seam-side down on a baking sheet and brush the top with warm margarine or butter. Cover with waxed paper.

13. Continue making triangles until the first half of the *filo* and half the filling is used.

14. Remove the unused portion of the *filo* from the refrigerator. Lay it flat and cover with waxed paper and a dampened dish towel.

    **Note:** This *filo* will be used to make pinwheels or snail shapes, which require *very* fresh pastry. If the *filo* breaks when twisted, it is not fresh enough and should be used to make more triangles or saved to make a large pie.

15. Remove one sheet of *filo* and experiment with it to determine the size of pinwheel desired. Cut the *filo* into several 4'' x 5'' and 5'' x 6'' pieces, and brush them with melted margarine or butter.

16. Place one piece with the long side facing you. Distribute 1 teaspoon of filling in a ridge about 1'' in from the long edge and both ends. Fold the long edge over the filling and then roll up the pastry like a jelly roll.

17. Beginning at one end, coil the roll tightly into a flat snail shape. Place the coil on a cookie sheet and brush the top with margarine or butter. Cover with a large sheet of waxed paper.

18. Preheat the oven to 350 F.

19. Choose the size of coil you prefer and cut, fill and roll the remaining *filo* leaves accordingly until all of the *filo* has been used up.

20. Bake the *tyropitakia* in the preheated oven for 15 to 18 minutes, or until crisp and puffy. Serve hot.

**Note:** These appetizers may be frozen before baking. Place them close to one another, in alternating layers with waxed paper, in a large box or container. When ready to bake, place the frozen *tyropitakia* on cookie sheets. They will require slightly longer to bake when frozen.

# SPANAKOPITA (SPINACH-FILO ROLLS)

## Matt Kramer

Four 12"-long rolls

A hearty Greek dish, *spanakopita* (the accent is on the "ko") reflects the lack of grazing land in Greece. The products of cows, goats and sheep are more often eaten than the animals themselves. In ancient times, meat, wine and even good bread were considered luxuries, and cheese was practically the only source of protein.

3 TO 4 POUNDS FRESH SPINACH,
OR 4 TO 5 PACKAGES FROZEN
CHOPPED SPINACH, THOROUGHLY
DRAINED
4 ONIONS, DICED
1 BUNCH SCALLIONS, CHOPPED
(WHITE AND GREEN PARTS)
¾ POUND (3 STICKS) BUTTER, PRE-
FERABLY UNSALTED

½ CUP MINCED PARSLEY
DILL (OPTIONAL)
1 POUND *FETA* CHEESE
1 CUP FRESHLY GRATED PARMESAN
8 EGGS, BEATEN
SALT
PEPPER
1 PACKAGE (1 POUND) *FILO* LEAVES

1. If you are using fresh spinach, remove the stems and plunge the leaves into boiling water for 5 minutes. Drain, squeeze out the liquid and coarsely chop the spinach. Set it aside.

2. In a large, heavy skillet, sauté the onions and scallions in 4 tablespoons of the butter until the onions are golden.

3. Add the parsley and dill (if using), and sauté for another 5 minutes.

4. Add the chopped spinach, sauté for an additional 5 to 10 minutes and empty the mixture into a large bowl. Set it aside to cool.

5. Crumble the *feta* cheese over the cooled spinach filling. Add the grated Parmesan, stir well and then fold in the beaten eggs. Add salt and pepper to taste.

6. Preheat the oven to 350 F.

7. Butter two baking sheets and set them aside.

8. Melt the remaining butter.

9. Place one leaf of *filo* on a flat surface and brush the top with melted butter. Place another leaf of *filo* on top of the first and brush it with butter. Repeat until you have a stack of five leaves.

   **Note:** *Filo* tends to dry out very quickly so it's a good idea to cover the sheets you are not actually using with a damp cloth or towel.

10. Spread one-fourth of the filling along one short edge of the *filo*, leaving 2" free on the sides. Fold the sides in over the filling and then roll the *filo* like a jelly roll.

11. Repeat the process to make three more spinach rolls.

12. Place the rolls seam-side down on the baking sheets and brush the tops with butter. Bake for about 1 hour, or until the crust is golden brown.

13. Allow the *spanakopita* to cool slightly, then slice and serve.

**Note:** You can change the proportions of spinach to cheese as you like in this recipe, and, if you don't like *feta*, you can substitute cottage cheese or mix the cheeses in equal proportions. Also, you can make the *spanakopita* in a cake pan or pie dish, using five layers of *filo* each for the top and bottom. The pie can then be cut into different bite-sized shapes like squares or triangles to serve as appetizers.

# CURRY TURNOVERS

Florence S. Lin

About 5 dozen

These turnovers can be made with either a meat or shrimp filling. To use both fillings, make two recipes of pastry.

**Meat Filling:**
2 TO 4 TABLESPOONS PEANUT OR
  CORN OIL
1 POUND (ABOUT 2 CUPS) GROUND
  PORK OR BEEF
1½ TABLESPOONS SOY SAUCE
2 TEASPOONS SALT
1½ TEASPOONS SUGAR
1 CUP MINCED ONION
2 TEASPOONS MADRAS CURRY
  POWDER
½ CUP PACKED MASHED POTATOES

1. Heat a wok over moderate heat until hot.

2. Add 1 tablespoon of the oil and the pork. (If beef is used, add 2 more tablespoons oil.) Stir-fry the meat until it separates into bits.

3. Add the soy sauce, salt and sugar; stir and mix well. Remove the meat from the wok and set aside.

4. In the same wok, heat 1 tablespoon of oil. Add the minced onion and stir-fry until it wilts, then add the curry powder. Stir and cook for 1 minute.

5. Add the cooked meat and the mashed potatoes. Stir and mix thoroughly. Let the mixture cool, and refrigerate to chill.

**Shrimp Filling:**
1 POUND FRESH OR FROZEN SHRIMP
  (ANY SIZE), THOROUGHLY THAWED
1 CUP FINELY MINCED ONION
3 TABLESPOONS LARD OR VEGE-
  TABLE SHORTENING
2 TEASPOONS MADRAS CURRY
  POWDER
1 TABLESPOON SALT
1 TEASPOON SUGAR
¼ TEASPOON MONOSODIUM GLU-
  TAMATE (MSG)
½ CUP PACKED MASHED POTATOES

1. Cover the shrimp with water and bring just to the boiling point, for baby shrimp. For larger shrimp, cook until pink.

2. Drain the shrimp, then grind or chop them finely and put into a mixing bowl.

3. In a wok or frying pan, stir-fry the onion in the lard (or vegetable shortening) until it wilts, add the curry powder, and stir together for 1 minute.

*Continued from preceding page*

4. Pour the onion mixture into the bowl with the shrimp, and add and mix in the remaining ingredients. Let cool and then refrigerate to chill.

**Pastry:**
2 LEVEL CUPS ALL-PURPOSE FLOUR
⅔ CUP SHORTENING OR LARD
⅓ CUP ICE WATER, APPROXIMATELY

1 EGG, BEATEN

1. While the shrimp or meat mixture is chilling, make the pastry. In a large mixing bowl, combine the flour with the shortening (or lard) and work with your fingertips until the shortening is evenly mixed in and the mixture is the consistency of cornmeal. Stir in the ⅓ cup of ice water, mix and pat into two balls. If the mixture seems too dry, sprinkle on a little more ice water.

2. Preheat the oven to 400 F.

3. On a lightly floured surface, roll out the dough, one ball at a time, into a large circle about ¹/₁₆'' thick.

4. Using a round cookie cutter, cut out 3''-diameter circles. Knead the scraps into a ball, roll out, and make more circles. Repeat until all the dough has been used.

5. Place about 1 heaping teaspoon of filling in the center of each dough circle, fold it over into a half-moon shape, and seal the edges tightly, crimping them by hand into a decorative scalloped pattern. If you prefer, you can also crimp the edges with a fork.

6. Place the turnovers on an ungreased baking sheet and prick each with a fork. Brush the tops with the beaten egg and bake in the preheated oven for about 20 minutes.

# CHEESE STRAWS

**Nan Mabon**

5½ dozen

½ POUND SHARP CHEDDAR CHEESE,
  GRATED
8 TABLESPOONS (1 STICK) BUTTER,
  SOFTENED
1¾ CUPS SIFTED FLOUR
½ TEASPOON SALT
¼ TEASPOON CAYENNE PEPPER
½ TEASPOON TABASCO SAUCE

1. In a bowl, beat together the cheese and butter until well blended.

2. Sift the flour along with the salt and cayenne directly into the cheese-butter mixture, add the Tabasco sauce, then mix well until thoroughly blended. Form the dough into two large patties, cover and refrigerate for 1 hour.

3. Preheat the oven to 425 F.

4. One at a time, roll out the two portions of dough until they are about $\frac{1}{8}$'' thick. Cut the dough into 5'' x $\frac{1}{2}$'' strips and carefully place the strips on cookie sheets.

5. Bake the cheese straws for 8 minutes. Then remove them from the oven and let them cool. If you are not serving the cheese straws immediately, store them in an airtight container.

Note: I personally prefer these cheese straws warm from the oven so I keep some dough on hand in the freezer and roll out only as many as will be needed for a particular occasion.

---

# CHEESE PUFFS (LA GOUGÈRE)

**Mireille Johnston**

12 servings

1 CUP PLUS 1 TABLESPOON MILK
7 TABLESPOONS BUTTER
1 CUP UNBLEACHED FLOUR
4 EGGS
1 CUP SWISS CHEESE, CUT INTO
   $\frac{1}{4}$'' DICE

1 TABLESPOON DIJON-STYLE MUS-
   TARD
PINCH OF NUTMEG
SALT, TO TASTE
FRESHLY GROUND WHITE PEPPER,
   TO TASTE

1. Preheat the oven to 400 F.

2. Butter a baking sheet.

3. Bring 1 cup of the milk to a boil and add 6 tablespoons of butter. When the butter has melted, remove the pan from the heat and add the flour all at once, stirring vigorously with a big wooden spoon. After a few minutes, when the mixture no longer clings to the sides of the pan, return it to the heat for 2 minutes.

4. Off the heat, beat in the eggs one by one, stirring constantly until the mixture is smooth and shiny. Pour in three-quarters of the cheese, all the mustard, nutmeg, salt and pepper. Taste carefully for seasoning; the *gougère* should not be bland.

5. To make individual puffs, drop the mixture from a spoon in dollops (about 1'' in diameter) spaced 2'' apart onto the prepared baking sheet.

6. Smooth the top of each one with a spatula or the back of a spoon and brush it with a little milk. Sprinkle the *gougères* with the rest of the cheese.

7. Place the *gougère* in the preheated oven and immediately turn down the temperature to 375 F. Bake for 25 minutes, then turn off the heat, set the oven door ajar and let them sit for 5 minutes. The top of each *gougère* should be quite firm to the touch.

Note: If you wish to make a large crown of pastry, make a 9'' ring by dropping spoonsful of the mixture onto a large, buttered baking sheet. Pile tablespoon over tablespoon of dough to make a high crown. Brush the top with milk and sprinkle

*Continued from preceding page*

with the remainder of the cheese. Bake in a 375 F. oven for 45 minutes. Turn off the oven, set the oven door ajar and let the *gougère* sit for 5 minutes. Again, the top of the *gougère* crown should be firm to the touch.

# SAUSAGE IN BRIOCHE

Susan Lipke

16 rolls

*Brioche:*
0.6 OUNCE (ABOUT ONE-THIRD OF A
  2-OUNCE CAKE) FRESH YEAST
1 TABLESPOON WARM WATER
1 TABLESPOON MILK
1 TABLESPOON SUGAR
1½ TEASPOONS SALT
10 OUNCES (ABOUT 2 CUPS) ALL-
  PURPOSE FLOUR
3 EGGS
½ POUND (2 STICKS) UNSALTED
  BUTTER, SLIGHTLY SOFTENED

*Sausage:*
¾ POUND FINE-TEXTURED FRESH
  PORK SAUSAGE, AT LEAST 1" IN
  DIAMETER
¾ CUP DRY WHITE WINE
½ TEASPOON SALT
1 BAY LEAF

1 EGG BEATEN WITH SEVERAL DROPS
  OF WATER

1. First make the *brioche*. In a small bowl, mash the yeast together with the warm water. Set it aside.

2. In the large bowl of an electric mixer equipped with a dough hook, combine the milk, sugar and salt, stirring to dissolve the granules with a wooden spoon.

3. Add the flour to the bowl, then scrape the yeast mixture onto the flour. Turn the mixer to low speed and beat the ingredients together for a moment, then add 2 of the eggs. Beat until the eggs are incorporated, then add the third egg. When it is incorporated, turn the mixer to medium speed and knead the dough for 15 minutes.

4. While the dough is being kneaded, prepare the butter. Place it between two sheets of waxed paper and roll it, beating if necessary, until it is malleable but not mushy.

5. When the dough is ready, turn the mixer back down to low speed and start adding the butter in pieces, waiting until one piece is incorporated before adding the next. When all the butter has been added and the mixture is well blended, scrape the dough into a buttered 1¾- to 2-quart mixing bowl, cover with plastic wrap and allow it to rise until doubled in size, about 1½ hours.

   **Note:** The dough will be quite sticky. Do not yield to the temptation to add more flour.

6. Punch the dough down in the bowl, cover and put it in the refrigerator for the second rising. If you want to leave the *brioche* dough for several hours or

overnight, weight the top of the bowl to prevent the dough from rising too much.

7. When ready to prepare the *brioche*, punch down the chilled dough, turn it onto a lightly floured surface and knead for a moment. Divide the dough into 16 equal parts, shape into balls and place on a baking sheet. Cover and return to the refrigerator while preparing the sausage.

8. Prick the sausage and place it in a saucepan with the wine, salt, bay leaf and enough water to cover. Bring to a boil, reduce the heat to a simmer, cover partially and poach for 20 to 25 minutes.

9. Butter 16 muffin cups.

10. Take the sheet of *brioche* dough from the refrigerator; remove 1 sausage at a time from the poaching liquid, peel it, if necessary, and cut into approximately 1½'' lengths.

    **Note:** Try to keep the sausage as hot as possible. If the *brioche* dough is wrapped around it while still hot, there is less likelihood of an air space developing around the sausage as the roll cooks.

11. One by one, flatten the balls of *brioche* dough into ovals, place a piece of sausage in the center, fold the ends of the oval over it so they overlap and pinch closed. Place the *brioche* seam-side down in a muffin cup. Repeat with the remaining ingredients.

    **Note:** The sausage will sink as the rolls cook, so the bottom layer of dough should be much thicker than the top.

12. Let the rolls rise until they reach above the tops of the muffin tins, about 1 hour.

13. Preheat the oven to 425 F.

14. Brush the rolls with the egg wash and bake in the preheated oven for 10 minutes, then reduce the heat to 375 F. and bake 10 minutes longer. Serve immediately.

# Fritters and Other Fried Hors d'Oeuvres

---

## VEGETABLE FRITTERS (PAKORAS)

**Satish Sehgal**

7 to 8 servings

Batter:
1 CUP CHICK-PEA FLOUR*, SIFTED
1 CUP WATER
½ TEASPOON SALT
½ TEASPOON CAYENNE PEPPER
½ TEASPOON *GARAM MASALA** OR
   ALLSPICE
¼ TEASPOON BAKING SODA

Other Ingredients:
3 MEDIUM-SIZED POTATOES, PEELED
   AND CUT INTO $1/_{16}$''-THICK ROUNDS,

OR 1 HEAD OF CAULIFLOWER BRO-
KEN INTO 1'' FLOWERETS, OR 1
LARGE EGGPLANT CUT INTO $1/_8$''-
THICK ROUNDS OR A COMBINATION
OF ALL THREE VEGETABLES
½ TEASPOON GROUND CORIANDER
½ TEASPOON GROUND CUMIN
¼ TEASPOON SALT
¼ TEASPOON CAYENNE PEPPER
VEGETABLE OIL

1. Put the chick-pea flour in a mixing bowl, add ½ cup of the water and blend to form a thick batter. Add the remaining water and beat for 10 minutes.

2. Add the salt, cayenne, *garam masala* (or allspice) and baking soda and mix well. Set the batter aside to rest for 15 minutes.

3. Meanwhile, place the cut vegetables in a large bowl and sprinkle them with the coriander, cumin, salt and cayenne. Toss until the vegetables are evenly coated.

4. Pour enough oil into a wok or deep-frying pan to reach a depth of 3'' and heat it to the smoking point. Lower the heat to medium. Take a few pieces of the vegetables and dip them in the batter. Drop the vegetables into the hot oil and fry, turning the fritters frequently, until they are golden brown on all sides. Remove them with a slotted spoon and drain on paper towels. Continue in this manner until all of the vegetables have been used.

5. Serve hot with mint chutney or tomato ketchup.

**Note:** *Pakoras* can also be prepared ahead of time and then refried before serving. To do this, the *pakoras* should be only partially cooked in the first frying, and then cooked until golden in the second frying.

* These ingredients are available in Indian markets.

---

# BITTER-BALLEN

## Matt Kramer

15 to 20 balls

I discovered *bitter-ballen* in a country tavern in Holland, where they are consumed in great quantity by local farmhands stopping off for a beer at the end of the day. For a number of guests, it is best to increase the following recipe and have the *bitter-ballen* ready in the refrigerator for last-minute frying.

2 CUPS PLUS 2 TABLESPOONS WATER
SALT
2 TO 3 SPRIGS PARSLEY
¼ ONION, SLICED
½ CARROT, SLICED
½ POUND VEAL, IN ONE PIECE (AN INEXPENSIVE CUT IS FINE)
4 TABLESPOONS (½ STICK) BUTTER
⅓ CUP FLOUR

½ TABLESPOON UNFLAVORED GELATIN
PEPPER
FRESHLY GRATED NUTMEG
1 EGG, SEPARATED
DRY BREAD CRUMBS
OIL
STRONG PREPARED MUSTARD

1. In a small pot, bring 2 cups of water to a boil and add 1 teaspoon of salt, the parsley, onion and carrot.

2. Add the veal, making sure that it is completely covered with water. Lower the heat and simmer for 40 minutes, or until the veal is tender.

3. Remove the veal from the broth and grind it through the finest blade of a meat grinder, or chop it to a fine consistency in a food processor. Set the stock aside.

4. In a skillet placed over low heat, melt the butter, then slowly add the flour, stirring constantly. Continue to stir until the *roux* is very smooth.

5. Gradually add 1 cup of the reserved veal stock. Allow the sauce to simmer for about 10 minutes, stirring frequently.

6. Soften the gelatin in 2 tablespoons of water for 5 minutes.

7. Add the softened gelatin to the sauce and season with salt, pepper and freshly grated nutmeg to taste.

8. Beat and stir in the egg yolk.

9. Blend in the ground veal and spread the mixture on a plate or board to cool.

10. When cool and stiff, form the mixture into small (1'') balls.

11. Lightly beat the egg white.

12. Roll the meatballs in the bread crumbs, then in egg white, and once more in the bread crumbs. (At this point, the *bitter-ballen* can be stored in the refrigerator until needed.)

13. Fill a deep-fryer or deep saucepan with enough oil to float a number of *bitter-ballen*. Heat the oil to 350 F. and fry the *bitter-ballen* until golden brown. Drain them on paper towels.

14. Serve while still hot with a side dish of strong mustard.

# ITALIAN MEAT BALLS (POLPETTE)

## Eliza and Joshua Baer

4 servings

A *polpetta* is a general term in Italian for a meat ball or for a small amount of "pulp." *Polpette* are meat balls for all occasions: in sauces, in stews, by themselves or with pasta. These *polpette* are best as hot or cold hors d'oeuvres.

1 LARGE EGG
½ CUP MILK
2 THICK SLICES FRENCH BREAD
1 POUND FRESHLY GROUND CHUCK
¼ POUND DICED BAKED HAM OR
  *PROSCIUTTO*
½ CUP FRESHLY GRATED PARMESAN,
  APPROXIMATELY
3 CLOVES GARLIC, CHOPPED OR
  MASHED
3 SCALLIONS, CUT INTO THIN,
  DIAGONAL SLICES

DASH OF TABASCO SAUCE
DASH OF FRESHLY GRATED NUTMEG
¼ CUP CHOPPED FRESH PARSLEY
1 TABLESPOON CHOPPED FRESH
  BASIL
2 TO 3 CUPS FRESH BREAD CRUMBS
2 CUPS PEANUT OIL
4 TO 5 TABLESPOONS OLIVE OIL
1 DRIED, HOT RED PEPPER, CHOPPED
  INTO FLAKES

1. Preheat the oven to 300 F.

2. Beat the egg and the milk together until frothy. Soak the slices of French bread in the egg-milk mixture.

3. Combine the ground chuck with the ham, Parmesan, garlic, scallions, Tabasco, nutmeg, parsley and basil.

4. Break the milk-soaked bread into small chunks. Add it, along with the milk-egg mixture, to the ground chuck.

5. If the resulting mixture is too loose or runny, stir in more Parmesan and ½ cup of the bread crumbs.

6. Shape the *polpette* by patting them into slightly flat footballs, a little longer than they are wide. Roll the *polpette* one at a time in the bread crumbs.

7. In a deep cast-iron frying pan, heat the peanut and olive oils until they reach 350 F. to 375 F. Toss the hot pepper flakes into the oil and let them simmer for 1 minute before frying the *polpette*.

8. Fry the *polpette* five at a time. They will take 10 to 15 minutes to turn golden brown on both sides. While they fry, keep the *polpette* from touching one another and from touching the bottom of the pan.

9. When the *polpette* are a deep golden brown, transfer them to a cookie sheet and place in the preheated oven. When all the *polpette* have been fried, give the last batch a few minutes in the oven before serving them all together.

10. Serve the *polpette* with hot mustard and horseradish.

**Note:** If you want to make the *polpette* several hours in advance, do not refrigerate them; they will taste better at room temperature. If you have to refrigerate them, reheat before serving at 375 F.

# CHICKEN-SHRIMP TOAST

**Gloria Bley Miller**

32 triangles

1 WHOLE CHICKEN BREAST, SKINNED,
 BONED AND MINCED
¼ POUND RAW SHRIMP, SHELLED,
 DEVEINED AND MINCED
1 STALK CELERY, MINCED
1 SMALL WHITE ONION, MINCED
1 EGG, SEPARATED
2 TABLESPOONS CHICKEN FAT

1 TABLESPOON CORNSTARCH
1 TABLESPOON MEDIUM-DRY SHERRY
½ TEASPOON SALT
½ TEASPOON SUGAR
8 SLICES WHITE BREAD, NOT TOO
 FRESH
VEGETABLE OIL
½ HEAD LETTUCE, SHREDDED

1. In a bowl, combine the minced chicken, shrimp, celery and onion with the egg white, chicken fat, cornstarch, sherry, salt and sugar. Blend well.

2. Trim off and discard the bread crusts, and cut each slice of bread into four triangles. Spread with the chicken-shrimp mixture, dipping the knife in water occasionally to prevent sticking.

3. Beat the egg yolk and brush it over the spread as a glaze.

4. Pour enough oil into a wok or deep-fryer to reach a depth of 2'' and heat it until nearly smoking. Add the prepared bread triangles, spread side down, a few at a time. Reduce the heat to medium and fry until the spread turns pinkish, about 3 minutes. Turn with tongs or a spatula and lightly brown the other side. Drain on paper towels and keep warm until all the triangles are done.

5. Transfer to a bed of the shredded lettuce and serve.


# GINGER PORK BALLS

**Maria Luisa Scott and Jack Denton Scott**

6 to 8 servings

We found these Cantonese hors d'oeuvres in Hong Kong, where they are very popular.

1½ POUNDS GROUND LEAN PORK
1 EGG, BEATEN
½ CUP MINCED WATER CHESTNUTS
1½ TABLESPOONS SOY SAUCE
1 TEASPOON SALT
1½ TABLESPOONS GRATED FRESH
 GINGER
½ CUP FINE DRY BREAD CRUMBS
PEANUT OIL

1. In a bowl, blend the pork, egg, water chestnuts, soy sauce, salt, ginger and

*Continued from preceding page*

bread crumbs. Form the mixture into small, compact balls.

2. In a wok or deep fryer, heat sufficient oil to cover the pork balls. Add the pork balls and fry until they are evenly browned.

3. Drain the pork balls on paper towels and serve them on toothpicks, accompanied by a dipping sauce of your choice. The Chinese usually serve a heavy soy sauce.

# FRIED FONTINA

## Nicola Zanghi

**4 servings**

A Piedmontese specialty, this appetizer is found in many restaurants. The fontina with brown rind tastes of the rich truffles that are produced in the same region of Italy. For this reason, only the true Piedmont fontina should be used.

1½ POUNDS FONTINA D'ALBA
VEGETABLE OIL
OLIVE OIL
FRESHLY GROUND BLACK PEPPER
FLOUR
3 EGGS, WELL BEATEN
FINE DRY BREAD CRUMBS

1. Cut the fontina into finger-like strips.

2. Pour the vegetable and olive oils in equal amounts into a heavy, deep saucepan, until they reach a depth of about 1''. Heat the oil until it has a light haze above it.

3. Meanwhile, sprinkle the cheese with pepper. Then dip each strip, first in flour to thoroughly coat it, then in the beaten egg and finally in bread crumbs.

4. Test the oil to make sure it will not burn the strips by first cooking a small piece of cheese in it. Then place a number of the strips in the hot oil and fry them until golden brown.

5. Remove the cheese fingers from the oil with a slotted spoon or wire skimmer, pat them dry with paper towels and serve immediately.

# FRITTATA AROMATICA

## Eliza and Joshua Baer

4 to 5 servings

This is one of many *frittate* (flat omelets) served as *antipasto* all over Italy.

3 TABLESPOONS BUTTER
1 TEASPOON FINELY CHOPPED
   FRESH THYME
1 FRESH MINT LEAF, VERY FINELY
   CHOPPED
1 TEASPOON FINELY CHOPPED
   FRESH TARRAGON
1 TEASPOON FINELY CHOPPED
   FRESH MARJORAM LEAVES
2 SCALLIONS, CUT INTO THIN,
   DIAGONAL SLICES

¼ CUP FINELY CHOPPED PARSLEY
6 EGGS
PINCH OF CAYENNE PEPPER
½ TEASPOON SALT
¼ TEASPOON BLACK PEPPER
FRESHLY GRATED NUTMEG, TO TASTE
½ CUP FRESHLY GRATED PARMESAN
2 TABLESPOONS DRY SOURDOUGH
   BREAD CRUMBS

1. Preheat the oven to 350 F.

2. In a 9'' ovenproof frying pan, melt the butter and sauté the thyme, mint, tarragon, marjoram and scallions for 3 minutes. Add the parsley.

3. Meanwhile, crack the eggs into a large bowl. Beat them vigorously with a whip and, as you beat them, add the cayenne, salt, black pepper, nutmeg, Parmesan and bread crumbs. The mixture will be thick and frothy.

4. Pour the egg mixture into the frying pan with the herbs. The butter should be hot, but not burning. Let the pan sit on high heat for 2 minutes, then place it in the preheated oven.

5. Check the *frittata* after 20 to 25 minutes. When done, the *frittata* should be golden brown on top, puffed slightly, like a quiche, and firm.

6. Remove the *frittata* from the oven. Let it cool for 10 to 20 minutes.

   **Note:** If the *frittata* is not to be served immediately, it can be refrigerated once it is cool.

7. Five minutes before serving, remove the *frittata* from the frying pan and place it on a cutting board. With a sharp knife, cut the *frittata* in half, then slice the halves into thin strips.

8. Arrange the strips on the cutting board, or on a platter, and serve with other classic *antipasto* dishes such as *prosciutto* and melon, marinated peppers and olives.

**Note:** For a more filling *frittata*, add 1 cup of marinated artichoke hearts and/or 1 cup of sliced, cooked zucchini to the ingredients in Step 2.

# CLAM FRITTERS

**Ruth Spear**

About 3 dozen

1½ CUPS FLOUR
½ TEASPOON SALT
6 TABLESPOONS (¾ STICK) BUTTER
3 EGGS, SEPARATED
¾ CUP BEER
24 FRESH CHERRYSTONE CLAMS,
  SHUCKED, DRAINED AND FINELY
  CHOPPED
1 TABLESPOON FINELY CHOPPED
  PARSLEY
1 TABLESPOON SNIPPED CHIVES
2 TABLESPOONS VEGETABLE OIL
LEMON WEDGES (OPTIONAL)
PARSLEY SPRIGS (OPTIONAL)

1. Sift the flour and salt into a mixing bowl.

2. Melt 4 tablespoons of the butter and stir in.

3. Beat the egg yolks lightly and add.

4. Gradually blend in the beer and let this batter stand in a warm place for about 1 hour.

5. Add the clams, parsley and chives to the batter.

6. Beat the egg whites until stiff, stir a small amount into the batter and then fold in the rest.

7. In a heavy skillet, heat the remaining 2 tablespoons of butter with the oil. When hot, drop in the batter by the tablespoon. Brown the fritters lightly on both sides and drain on paper towels.

8. Serve hot, as an hors d'oeuvre or as a first course, garnished with lemon wedges and parsley, if desired.

# Vegetable, Egg and Seafood Appetizers

---

## MUSHROOMS STUFFED WITH PROSCIUTTO

**Nicola Zanghi**

4 servings

These stuffed mushroom hors d'oeuvres can also be served as part of a hot *antipasto*, as cocktail snacks, or with *aperitifs*.

24 EXTRA-LARGE MUSHROOMS
1 LEMON
½ CUP DRY WHITE WINE
½ CUP CLARIFIED BUTTER
¼ CUP MINCED SCALLIONS (WHITE PART ONLY)
¼ POUND *PROSCIUTTO*, FINELY MINCED
½ TEASPOON OREGANO
¼ CUP GRATED PARMESAN
¼ CUP FINELY DICED SWISS CHEESE
2 HARD-COOKED EGGS, FINELY CHOPPED
3 TABLESPOONS CHOPPED PARSLEY
1 EGG, LIGHTLY BEATEN
6 GRINDS OF BLACK PEPPER

1. Preheat the oven to 400 F.

2. Remove the stems from the mushrooms and reserve them. Rub the caps with the lemon to prevent discoloration.

3. In a shallow pan, poach the caps, stem-side up for 5 minutes, in a mixture of half the wine and half the clarified butter. Do *not* overcook. Remove the caps from the pan and keep them warm.

4. Mince the reserved mushroom stems and set aside.

5. Heat the remaining ¼ cup of butter in another pan, add the scallions and sauté them over moderate heat until limp.

6. Add the *prosciutto* and sauté for 5 minutes.

7. Add the mushroom stems and sauté for 5 minutes more, stirring constantly.

8. Add the remaining ¼ cup of wine, and cook to reduce the liquid to one-third of its volume.

9. Transfer the cooked *prosciutto* mixture to a bowl. Add the remaining ingredients and mix well.

    **Note:** A food processor or blender comes in extremely handy for this step.

10. Fill the mushroom caps with the stuffing.

11. Transfer the stuffed caps to a baking dish and bake in the preheated oven for 10 minutes. If more browning is desired, place the caps briefly under the broiler.

---

# SHRIMP SCANDIA

**Maurice Moore-Betty**

6 servings

Sauce:
1 TABLESPOON PREPARED MUSTARD
1 TABLESPOON SUGAR
1½ TABLESPOONS WINE VINEGAR
½ TEASPOON SALT
1 TABLESPOON FINELY CHOPPED
    PARSLEY
WHITE PEPPER, TO TASTE
1 TEASPOON LEMON JUICE
1 TEASPOON CHOPPED FRESH DILL
¼ CUP SALAD OIL

Shrimp:
1½ POUNDS SHRIMP (25 TO 30 TO
    THE POUND)
2 TABLESPOONS FINELY CHOPPED
    ONION
1 STALK CELERY, FINELY CHOPPED
1 TABLESPOON SALT
4 PEPPERCORNS

1. Shell and devein the shrimp. Then rinse under cold running water.

2. In a heavy pan, combine the onion, celery, salt, peppercorns and enough water to cover the shrimp when they are added.

3. Bring the water to a boil, reduce the heat and simmer, covered, for 5 minutes. Add the shrimp and bring to a boil again.

4. Remove the pan from the heat and let the shrimp stand for 2 to 3 minutes. Drain and let them cool.

5. Combine all of the sauce ingredients in a bottle and shake well.

6. Toss the shrimp with the sauce and allow to stand for several hours. Serve the marinated shrimp on toothpicks.

# STUFFED ARTICHOKE HEARTS AND MUSHROOM CAPS

**Florence Fabricant**

6 servings

12 MUSHROOM CAPS, 2" IN DIAMETER
9 TABLESPOONS OLIVE OIL
12 ARTICHOKE BOTTOMS, 1½" IN
    DIAMETER, COOKED UNTIL TENDER*
2 TABLESPOONS WINE VINEGAR
1 TEASPOON DIJON MUSTARD
½ TEASPOON SALT
FRESHLY GROUND BLACK PEPPER,
    TO TASTE
⅔ CUP SOUR CREAM
2 OUNCES BLACK CAVIAR

1. Sauté the mushroom caps in 3 tablespoons of the olive oil until well coated. Drain on paper towels.

2. In a bowl, combine the artichoke bottoms and the mushroom caps.

3. Mix the remaining 6 tablespoons of oil with the vinegar, mustard, salt and pepper and pour over the mushrooms and artichokes. Allow to marinate for about 12 hours, tossing from time to time.

4. Drain the mushrooms and artichoke bottoms and pat dry.

5. Put about 1½ teaspoons of the sour cream into each mushroom cap and on each artichoke bottom, and top each with about ½ teaspoon caviar. Arrange on a platter and serve.

\* If canned artichoke bottoms are used, they should be rinsed and dried before marinating. Canned, *marinated* artichoke bottoms may also be used. In that case, however, marinate only the mushrooms and add the artichokes after the mushrooms have marinated.

# SWEET RED PEPPER AND BASIL SPIRALS

## Elizabeth Schneider Colchie

About 32 spirals

4 VERY LARGE, STRAIGHT-SIDED
  RED BELL PEPPERS
¾ CUP CHOPPED, LIGHTLY PACKED
  FRESH BASIL LEAVES
3 TO 4 TABLESPOONS OLIVE OIL
2 TABLESPOONS CHOPPED PINE NUTS
1 SMALL CLOVE GARLIC, MINCED
½ TEASPOON SALT
½ TEASPOON PEPPER
BLACK OLIVES (OPTIONAL)

1. Spear the peppers on a long kitchen fork and hold them directly over a gas flame, turning them frequently, until they are charred on all sides and top and bottom.

2. While still hot, remove the stem, slice the peppers lengthwise into eighths and scrape off the skin and seeds with a sharp paring knife. Dry the pieces on paper towels.

3. In the container of a blender or food processor, combine the basil, olive oil, pine nuts, garlic, salt and pepper, and make a fine purée. Stop the machine often to push the mixture down the sides, if you are using a blender. Taste for seasoning.

4. Spread a thin layer of the paste on the inside of each pepper strip.

5. Roll each strip up tightly starting from the narrow end and secure it with a toothpick. Arrange the strips on a platter with oil-cured, black olives, if desired.

# MARINATED MUSHROOMS

## Jane Moulton

About 10 servings

30 SMALL WHITE PICKLING ONIONS
  OR 30 WHITE SCALLION STALKS
1 POUND MEDIUM-LARGE FIRM, WHITE
  FRESH MUSHROOMS, CLEANED
  AND TRIMMED
1 CUP RED WINE VINEGAR
1 CUP VEGETABLE OIL

1 TABLESPOON DRIED TARRAGON
1 TABLESPOON SUGAR
1½ TEASPOONS SALT
½ TEASPOON WHOLE SZECHUAN
  PEPPER
1 SMALL ONION, PEELED
2 CLOVES GARLIC, PEELED

1. Peel the onions (or trim the scallion stalks) and place them with the mushrooms in a glass, ceramic or stainless-steel bowl.

2. In the container of a blender or food processor, blend the remaining ingredients until smooth.

3. Pour the blended mixture over the mushrooms and onions and refrigerate for 24 hours, stirring the marinade occasionally.

4. Just before serving, remove the mushrooms and onions from the marinade with a slotted spoon, taking as many as are needed for the first serving and leaving the remainder in the marinade. Drain briefly on paper towels and serve with toothpicks.


# TEA EGGS

## Gloria Bley Miller

6 to 8 servings

10 EGGS
¼ CUP SOY SAUCE
¼ CUP BLACK TEA LEAVES
1½ TEASPOONS SALT

1½ TEASPOONS CINNAMON
4 CUPS WATER
PARSLEY

1. In a pan, place the eggs with water to cover and bring slowly to a boil. Reduce the heat and cook another 10 minutes, until hard cooked.

2. Cool the cooked eggs under cold running water and drain. Tap each egg lightly with the back of a spoon to crack the entire shell, but do not peel.

3. In a pan, combine the soy sauce, tea, salt, cinnamon and water. Bring to a boil, reduce the heat, cover, and let the mixture simmer for 10 minutes to blend the flavors.

4. Add the eggs in their cracked shells, cover, and simmer for 1 hour. The eggs should be covered by the liquid: If not, turn them once or twice.

5. Cool the eggs in the liquid. Shell only when ready to serve. Serve them whole or halved, garnished with the parsley.

# Hot Meat Appetizers

## CHICKEN LAULAUS

**Maria Luisa Scott and Jack Denton Scott**

8 servings

Pork or fish is sometimes used instead of the chicken breasts in this popular Hawaiian hors d'oeuvre, which each guest unfolds himself, eating the tasty offering with either a fork or his fingers.

1 POUND SALT PORK, DICED
2 POUNDS BONED CHICKEN BREASTS,
   CUT INTO ½" CUBES
2 POUNDS SWISS CHARD*, CUT INTO
   1" x ¼" STRIPS
12 YOUNG SCALLIONS (WHITE PART
   ONLY), MINCED
SALT, TO TASTE
HUSKS OF 8 LARGE EARS OF CORN
BOILING WATER

1. In a saucepan, sauté the salt pork until crisp.

2. Stir in the cubed chicken and cook for 5 minutes.

3. Add the Swiss chard and cook for 5 minutes.

4. Stir in the scallions, blend well and taste for salt, adding some if necessary.

5. Lay out eight 8" x 14" sheets of foil. Place the husks of one ear of corn in the middle of each sheet, with the leaves bisecting one another at the center, thus forming a solid circle.

   **Note:** In the Islands *ti* leaves are used, not foil. But corn husks and foil are good substitutes.

6. Place equal portions of the chicken mixture in the center of each arrangement of corn husks. Pull the four corners of the foil together, twisting them tightly to form a neat, secure bundle.

7. Place the foil bundles on a rack in a large pot and pour boiling water around them to a depth of 1". Cover the pot and simmer for 35 minutes.

8. Serve in the foil.

\* Hawaiian islanders use taro leaves or bok choy.

# ANDEAN TAMALES

**Jeanne Lesem**

About 10 *tamales*

I first tasted these *tamales* on a trip to Machu Picchu, the lost city of Peru, to which the Indians fled during the Spanish invasion. We bought some from a vendor at a cable-car stop at a village between Cuzco and Machu Picchu. They were slightly sweet, and though not even warm, they were unusually delicious. They can be served as snacks with a drink, as a first course at dinner, or as a main course at lunch. Traditionally the *tamales* are served at room temperature, but they can also be eaten hot.

5 CUPS WATER
1 CUP REGULAR (NOT INSTANT) HOMINY GRITS
1 TEASPOON SALT
¼ POUND MILD PORK SAUSAGE
½ POUND LEAN PORK
2 LARGE CLOVES GARLIC, CRUSHED
¼ TEASPOON WHOLE ANISEED
1 ONION, ABOUT 2'' IN DIAMETER, FINELY CHOPPED

ONE 4''-LONG FRESH CHILE PEPPER, STEMMED, SEEDED AND CUT INTO THIN STRIPS*
1 TO 2 HARD-COOKED EGGS, CUT INTO LENGTHWISE STRIPS
ABOUT 30 PEANUTS, ROASTED, SHELLED AND SKINNED

1. In a heavy, 2-quart saucepan, bring the water to a boil and slowly stir in the grits. Lower the heat, add the salt, cover and cook slowly for 25 to 30 minutes, stirring occasionally to prevent sticking.

2. Meanwhile, put the sausage, either whole or cut in half, into a cold frying pan, set it over medium heat, and cook until it begins to render a little fat.

3. Add the pork, either whole or cut into several pieces of equal thickness, and cook, turning occasionally, until the juices no longer run pink when the meat is pricked with a fork.

4. Add the garlic, aniseed, onion and pepper strips, stirring to brown and flavor the meat.

5. Turn off the heat; remove the meat from the pan with a slotted spoon and cut both the sausage and lean pork into ¼'' x 3'' strips. Set them aside on a plate together with the egg strips and peanuts.

6. With a wooden spoon, mix the pan drippings and fat into the cooked grits.

7. Cut lightweight aluminum foil into ten 10'' x 12'' strips.

8. Divide the grits into ten equal portions. Pat half of each portion into the shape of a long, narrow rectangle down the middle of a foil strip. Run a strip of pork and one of sausage down the center of the grits, leaving room at both ends. Top with 3 peanuts and 1 or 2 strips of egg.

9. Pat a half portion of grits over each strip of filling to completely cover it. Then seal the foil package by wrapping it like a sandwich at a take-out counter. Bring the two long sides of the foil together above the filling; fold them over several times to take up the slack in the foil. Make several small folds in the short ends, then fold them underneath the *tamale* package.

**Note:** At this point you can refrigerate the *tamales* for a few days, or freeze them for a couple of weeks in the freezer-top of a refrigerator or for a month or two in a freezer that goes down to zero degrees Fahrenheit.

10. When you are ready to cook the *tamales*, place them in a skillet large enough to hold them in a single layer, cover them with boiling water and cook gently for 2 to 2½ hours.

11. Remove the *tamales* from the water with a slotted spoon, cool to room temperature and serve right in the foil packets. If they are not firm enough to be eaten out of hand, as is the custom in Peru, use forks.

\* Be careful when seeding the peppers. If you have sensitive skin, use plastic or rubber gloves; avoid touching your eyes or lips until you have washed your hands.

# GLAZED HAM BALLS

## Ruth Ellen Church

12 servings

For years, these have been one of my party specialties. I often make a triple batch ahead of time and then freeze them for impromptu gatherings. I find that they go very quickly, so you may want to make more than one recipe's worth.

1½ POUNDS GROUND PORK
1½ POUNDS LEAN HAM, GROUND
1 CUP MILK
2 CUPS SOFT BREAD CRUMBS
1 TEASPOON SALT
1½ CUPS BROWN SUGAR
⅔ CUP RED WINE VINEGAR
1 CUP WATER
1 TABLESPOON HOT PREPARED
   MUSTARD

1. Preheat the oven to 325 F.

2. In a bowl, combine the ground meats with the milk, bread crumbs and salt. Mix well and shape into small balls, about 1'' in diameter. Place the balls in a deep ovenproof pan.

3. In a saucepan, bring the sugar, vinegar, water and mustard to a boil, stirring to dissolve the sugar.

4. Pour the sauce over the ham balls and bake in the preheated oven for 1 hour, basting generously now and then with the sauce.

5. If there is time, cool and then chill the ham balls, then remove the hardened fat that rises to the surface. Reheat the ham balls before serving.

Note: The ham balls will keep well for at least a week if well refrigerated. For a change of pace, a can (9 ounces) of crushed pineapple can be added to the glaze.

# POLYNESIAN BEEF

**Maurice Moore-Betty**

About 33 servings

1 BOTTLE (10 OUNCES) SOY SAUCE
1 BOTTLE (10 OUNCES) TERIYAKI
SAUCE (AVAILABLE IN ORIENTAL
MARKETS)
2 CLOVES GARLIC, PEELED AND
CHOPPED

ONE 3" STRIP FRESH GINGER,
COARSELY CHOPPED
1½ POUNDS FILLET OF BEEF, TRIM-
MED OF ALL FAT AND GRISTLE,
CUT INTO ¾" CUBES*
1 TABLESPOON UNSALTED BUTTER

1. In a heavy pan, bring the sauces, garlic and ginger to a boil and simmer gently for about 5 minutes. Set aside to cool.

2. Put the cubed beef into a glass or enamel dish and pour the marinade over it. Let stand for about 1 hour, turning several times.

3. In a heavy skillet, heat the butter, and, when almost smoking, sear the cubes of beef quickly on all sides. This should not take more than a minute.

4. Serve very hot on toothpicks.

**Note:** Any remaining marinade may be saved for later use; chicken, for example, is also delicious marinated in the sauce.

# LEMON-GLAZED SPARERIBS

**Emanuel and Madeline Greenberg**

8 to 10 servings

3 TO 4 POUNDS SPARERIBS, CUT
INTO 2" PIECES
¾ CUP WATER
½ CUP FRESH LEMON JUICE
¼ CUP SOY SAUCE
½ CUP SUGAR
1 TABLESPOON CORNSTARCH

½ TEASPOON SALT
¾ TEASPOON GRATED LEMON RIND
½ TEASPOON POWDERED GINGER
¼ TEASPOON PEPPER
2 CLOVES GARLIC, CRUSHED
½ TEASPOON LEMON EXTRACT

1. Preheat the oven to 350 F.

2. Line one or two shallow baking pans with heavy-duty aluminum foil and arrange the ribs in a single layer in the pan(s). Bake for 40 minutes, turning occasionally, and draining off the fat.

3. While the ribs are baking, make the glazing sauce. Combine all the remaining ingredients in a small saucepan. Bring to a boil, stirring often, turn down the heat and simmer for 3 minutes.

4. Pour about half the sauce over the ribs and bake for 20 minutes longer.

5. Turn the ribs and baste with the remaining sauce. Return the ribs to the oven and bake until they are well browned and glazed.

# LAMB PATTIES

## Satish Sehgal

6 servings

This dish is typical of the Muslim cuisine, which consists primarily of kebabs and other *moghlai* dishes so popular in Northern India. These dishes combine a variety of finely-ground spices and herbs and chopped meat, which are shaped into small round or oval patties and fried. In the Muslim neighborhoods of Indian cities, street vendors preparing these kebabs do a brisk roadside business.

1 CUP WATER
1 POUND CHOPPED LAMB
1 MEDIUM-SIZED ONION, MINCED
1 TEASPOON SALT
½ CUP DRIED YELLOW SPLIT PEAS
6 CLOVES GARLIC, PEELED AND
  MINCED
½ TEASPOON TURMERIC
½ TEASPOON CAYENNE PEPPER
ONE 1½" PIECE FRESH GINGER,
  PEELED AND MINCED

2 FRESH GREEN CHILE PEPPERS*,
  FINELY CHOPPED
½ TEASPOON *GARAM MASALA* OR
  ALLSPICE
1 TABLESPOON LIME JUICE
2 TABLESPOONS CHOPPED FRESH
  CORIANDER
1 EGG, LIGHTLY BEATEN
3 TABLESPOONS OIL, APPROXIMATELY

1. In a saucepan, heat the water and add the lamb, onion, salt, split peas, garlic, turmeric and cayenne. Stir, cover and cook over low heat for about 45 minutes. Uncover, raise the heat and cook rapidly until all the liquid has evaporated. Remove from the heat and cool.

2. Put the cooked meat through a grinder together with the ginger, chile peppers and *garam masala* (or allspice).

3. Add the lime juice, coriander and the egg to the ground mixture and mix thoroughly until the combined ingredients form a pliable and somewhat sticky mass.

4. Divide the mixture into 12 equal parts. Shape into rounds or ovals and flatten them into small patties.

5. In a skillet, heat the oil and fry the patties on both sides until golden brown. Add a little more oil, if necessary. Remove the patties with a slotted spoon and drain on paper towels.

6. Serve immediately with mint chutney and a relish of onions, ginger, green chile peppers and mint, sprinkled with fresh lime juice.

* These ingredients are available in Indian markets.

# SKEWERED CHICKEN AND ONION (YAKITORI)

**Mitsuo Masuzawa**

2 servings

*Teriyaki* Sauce:
½ CUP *MIRIN** (SWEET *SAKE*)
½ CUP JAPANESE SOY SAUCE*
½ CUP CHICKEN STOCK (FRESH OR
   CANNED)

Chicken:
½ POUND BONELESS CHICKEN LEG
½ POUND BONELESS CHICKEN
   BREAST
1 ONION
*KONASANSHO** (JAPANESE PEPPER)

1. In a 1-quart enameled- or stainless-steel saucepan, warm the *mirin* over moderate heat. When warm, turn off the heat and ignite the *mirin* with a match, then shake the pan back and forth until the flame dies out.

2. Stir in the soy sauce and chicken stock and bring to a boil.

3. Pour the sauce into a bowl and cool to room temperature.

4. Meanwhile, preheat the broiler or light a hibachi or charcoal grill.

5. Cut the chicken legs and breasts into 1'' pieces, making a total of approximately 24 pieces.

6. Cut the onion into ¾'' cubes.

7. Using six 8''-long bamboo skewers, alternate pieces of chicken with 3 cubes of onion on each skewer.

   **Note:** The bamboo skewer must not pass completely through the last piece of meat. The tip should remain unexposed.

8. Quickly dip the chicken and onion skewers in the *teriyaki* sauce and broil on one side for 2 to 3 minutes. Dip again in the sauce and continue to grill on the same side for 3 more minutes. Dip a third time and grill on the other side for an additional 3 minutes. The entire grilling should take 8 to 9 minutes altogether.

   **Note:** Do not allow the exposed ends of the skewers to burn since you will need to pick them up by these free ends.

9. Serve three skewers on a plate and sprinkle each skewer with a little *konasansho*, then moisten with a teaspoon of *teriyaki* sauce.

* Available in Oriental grocery stores.